Junkyard Sports

Bernie DeKoven

Human Kinetics

Library of Congress Cataloging-in-Publication Data

DeKoven, Bernie, 1941-
  Junkyard sports / Bernie DeKoven.
    p. cm.
  ISBN 0-7360-5207-0 (soft cover)
  1. Ball games. I. Title.
  GV861.D43 2005
  796.3--dc22   2004008987
ISBN-13: 978-0-7360-5207-8
ISBN-10: 0-7360-5207-0

The Web addresses cited in this text were current as of April 04, 2004, unless otherwise noted.

Acquisitions Editor: Gayle Kassing, PhD; **Developmental Editor:** Jennifer M. Sekosky; **Assistant Editors:** Ragen E. Sanner and Bethany J. Bentley; **Copyeditor:** Jan Feeney; **Proofreader:** Anne Rogers; **Graphic Designer:** Fred Starbird; **Graphic Artist:** Yvonne Griffith; **Photo Manager:** Kareema McLendon; **Cover Designer:** Andrea Souflée; **Photographer:** Kelly J. Huff; **Art Manager:** Kelly Hendren; **Illustrator:** Bob Gregson; **Printer:** Versa Press

Printed in the United States of America   10 9 8 7 6 5 4 3 2

Human Kinetics
Web site: www.HumanKinetics.com

United States: Human Kinetics, P.O. Box 5076, Champaign, IL 61825-5076
800-747-4457
e-mail: humank@hkusa.com

Canada: Human Kinetics, 475 Devonshire Road Unit 100, Windsor, ON N8Y 2L5
800-465-7301 (in Canada only)
e-mail: orders@hkcanada.com

Europe: Human Kinetics, 107 Bradford Road, Stanningley
Leeds LS28 6AT, United Kingdom
+44 (0) 113 255 5665
e-mail: hk@hkeurope.com

Australia: Human Kinetics, 57A Price Avenue, Lower Mitcham, South Australia 5062
08 8372 0999
e-mail: liaw@hkaustralia.com

New Zealand: Human Kinetics, Division of Sports Distributors NZ Ltd.
P.O. Box 300 226 Albany, North Shore City, Auckland
0064 9 448 1207
e-mail: info@humankinetics.co.nz

To my grandchildren, that they might find a world of sports that is healthier, more supportive, and more fun. To my children, who are working toward building that very world, in theater and design, childcare and childrearing. To my wife who brings me a daily life that is healthier, more supportive, and more fun.

In loving memory of my father, who taught me the value of games; my mother, who taught me the transcendence of love; Burton Naiditch, with whom I worked as co-director of the New Games Foundation and envelope stuffer; Ken Feit, the holy fool; Becca, who danced; and of all those workshoppers and playmates who taught me what it means to teach fun.

And especially you, because, forgive me, I don't know or didn't remember your name, and yet, without you, there'd be no reason for all this junk.

Contents

Idea Finder

Junkyard game	Game number	Based on	Page number
Ad Hoc Golf Soccer	4.6	Soccer	41
Air Basketball	6.8	Basketball	91
Air-Broom Hockey	8.6	Hockey	134
All-Terrain Basketball	6.5	Basketball	87
Ball-for-All Basketball	6.1	Basketball	80
Base Football	5.10	Football	71
Base-Tag Baseball	7.3	Baseball	105
Basebasket	6.10	Basketball	95
Beach-Basket Soccer	4.3	Soccer	36
Blind Robot Soccer	4.10	Soccer	48
Bocce-Box Soccer	4.8	Soccer	45
Bowl Hockey	8.11	Hockey	142
Box Baseball	7.12	Baseball	122
Broom Hockey	8.1	Hockey	124
Bumper Pool Hockey	8.5	Hockey	132
Chair Volley	9.9	Volleyball	162
Chariot Hockey	8.4	Hockey	130
Chess Football	5.7	Football	65
Chopsticky	8.8	Hockey	138
Cricket Bowling Baseball	7.6	Baseball	110
Dodgeball Baseball	7.1	Baseball	102
Everybody Has a Ball Hockey	8.9	Hockey	140
Foosball Soccer	4.12	Soccer	51
Frisbee Baseball	7.5	Baseball	108
Frisbee Hockey	8.3	Hockey	128
Golf Baseball	7.10	Baseball	118
Gollyball	9.5	Volleyball	156
Goodminton	9.6	Volleyball	158
Hallball	7.11	Baseball	120
Handless Volley	9.7	Volleyball	159
Hide-and-Seek Hockey	8.7	Hockey	136

Junkyard game	Game number	Based on	Page number
Hopping Soccer	4.9	Soccer	46
Kick-Bowl Soccer	4.4	Soccer	38
Kick-the-Can Football	5.11	Football	73
Kingvolley	9.2	Volleyball	150
Living-Room Volley	9.10	Volleyball	163
Marbles Soccer	4.1	Soccer	32
Musical Basketless Basketball	6.7	Basketball	90
Netless Volley	9.8	Volleyball	161
Noodle Hockey	8.2	Hockey	126
One-Foot Football	5.9	Football	69
Paper-Wad Basketball	6.9	Basketball	93
Pinball Soccer	4.11	Soccer	49
Playground Baseball	7.7	Baseball	112
Playground Basketball	6.6	Basketball	89
Poison-Sock Football	5.5	Football	61
Prisoner's Baseball	7.2	Baseball	103
Puck Puck	8.12	Hockey	144
Racket Basket	6.3	Basketball	83
Racketless Racquetball Soccer	4.7	Soccer	43
Rally Volley	9.1	Volleyball	148
Ring Around the Basketball	6.12	Basketball	98
Schmerltz Baseball	7.4	Baseball	106
Schmerltz Football	5.2	Football	56
Schmerltz Volley	9.13	Volleyball	168
Scoot Basketball	6.13	Basketball	100
Scooter Football	5.12	Football	75
Scrum Football	5.3	Football	58
Shufflehockey	8.10	Hockey	141
Skateboard Hockey	8.13	Hockey	145
Slip-and-Crawl Soccer	4.2	Soccer	34
Spoon Football	5.4	Football	60
Sugar-Pack Football	5.13	Football	77
Tennis Baseball	7.8	Baseball	113

(continued)

(continued)

Junkyard game	Game number	Based on	Page number
Three-Team Soccer	4.13	Soccer	52
Toilet-Paper Football	5.6	Football	63
Towely Volley	9.4	Volleyball	154
Trash Basketball	6.4	Basketball	85
Viking Soccer Football	5.1	Football	54
Volley Soccer	4.5	Soccer	39
Volleyall	9.11	Volleyball	165
Volleyvolley	9.12	Volleyball	167
Wall Basketball	6.11	Basketball	97
Water Balloony	9.3	Volleyball	152
Water Football	5.8	Football	67
Waterball	7.9	Baseball	116
Wheelchair Doubles Basketball	6.2	Basketball	81

Preface

Junkyard Sports emphasizes fun and creativity, teamwork and leadership, inclusion and adaptability, compassion and acceptance, humor, playfulness, and community. The activities are designed not only to engage mind and body but also to help participants develop the arts of collaboration and effective team building, acquire leadership, and experience the power and practicality of using problem solving and the scientific method.

The term *junkyard sports* is a play on a very successful TV series called *Junkyard Wars* that was shown on the TLC network. Like junkyard sports, *Junkyard Wars* is a team effort, requiring ingenuity and collaboration in the use of found materials. The similarity stops there. Junkyard sports are not wars or even competitions, and the purpose is not to build machines but to build community. However, the connection is strong enough to capture the spirit of this unique focus on sports.

Junkyard Sports is a collection of physical activities. Like most books of this genre, it is intended for use by recreation planners, youth leaders, and physical educators as a resource for new activities that can be implemented easily, with minimal preparation, and with high probability of success. Unlike most of these books, *Junkyard Sports* is not a collection of sports but a collection of activities that lead to the creation of sports. These sports are not necessarily for a particular age or ability level but for homogeneous or diverse groups of children and adults with a range of physical abilities and limitations.

Most game collections require a dependence on the inventiveness of others. Junkyard sports foster interdependence. Games in collections have to be adapted or modified for different populations. Junkyard sports are created by the populations who play them—by the players, for the players. As valuable as collections of cooperative and alternative sports are for the physical educator and the recreational or youth leader who must respond to the needs of various populations, there are never enough games, no matter how large or esoteric the collection. It is taxing to have to learn and teach a new sport, taxing again to have to find more and newer sports, and especially taxing to discover that these sports are really not enough. By themselves, they may be fun or meet certain objectives. But they rarely engage the spirit of playfulness, empower all of the players, stimulate creativity, or lead to the development of newer sports.

Junkyard Sports gives physical educators and recreation and youth leaders a rich, exciting, and growing resource for physical activities that will work in any environment, with any population. This book makes it easy for people to initiate completely new activities for any audience in five minutes or less.

This book is designed to give the reader starting points, or demonstration games, rather than instructions for playing specific sports. The bulk of the book is taken up by part two, "The Junkmasters' Guide," a collection of ideas for new, fun, and challenging invitations to sports. For example, when looking in the baseball section, you might see a baseball-like demonstration game played with a tennis racket for a bat, a beach ball for a ball, five traffic-cone bases, and the batter sitting on a gym scooter. In the next game, everyone in the field might carry a lacrosse stick, and there are two batters, both holding on to either end of a towel.

Each demonstration game really is a collection of innovative principles—ideas that can be used to create other demonstration games. Borrowing the gym-scooter idea, you suddenly have a new way to play soccer, basketball, football, or hockey. Every demonstration game gets refined as it gets played. Maybe the lacrosse sticks don't work as well as hockey sticks. Maybe a tricycle is more fun than a gym scooter. In refining the demonstration game, players create a new demonstration game, which in turn results in the creation of another and another.

WHY JUNKYARD SPORTS?

Ever since the success of the New Games concept, I've been troubled by the one part that never seemed to get accurately transmitted—the part about inventing your own sports. *Junkyard Sports* comes 30 years later. They're junkyard sports because the sports themselves are throwaway. They're junk compared to the treasured experience of inventing a sport that brought everything and everyone together in fun.

I'm interested in getting senior citizens, young people, and those with disabilities to play together. I'm interested in getting people to create junkyard sports for the triathlete to play with a person who uses a wheelchair, and the preschool child to play with the adult. I like sports where the focus is on playing together. I'm interested in celebrations of everyone's abilities.

As for "why now?," it seems to be time. Inability or unwillingness to adapt to change is killing people in retirement homes and demoralizing them in business and educational institutions. The use of public recreation facilities and parks is declining. More and more schools are outlawing recess. As more schools reduce the scope of physical education to sports and calisthenics, as more parents force their children into organized sports for which they have neither the skill nor the inclination, we find ourselves with a growing population of sedentary, obese, disenfranchised, isolated kids who lack basic physical and social skills. Entering the community and the workforce, these people find themselves unable to function as part of a team or to muster the physical and mental stamina necessary to reach their goals.

And so many physical educators, recreation leaders, therapists, and everyone else who loved New Games are in need of something newer, something just as inclusive and attractive and fun. So do people who have noticed that their world is changing faster and faster, and the abilities to adapt and include are becoming more strongly linked with survival.

Junkyard sports give people a way to have fun together. It really doesn't matter what they are playing. It definitely doesn't matter who wins what. What matters is that they are all engaged, challenged, involved, and enjoying themselves and each other. As far as they are concerned, fun is the whole reason for playing the sports. They are invitations for people to have fun with each other, with their bodies and abilities, minds and hearts. Junkyard sports are opportunities to create new, funny sports for which winning isn't the point. Playing together is.

Acknowledgments

Over the last 35 years of my exploration of ways to bring more fun to the world, several people have helped to sustain me, intellectually and spiritually. And indirectly, it's their presence in my heart and mind that has made this book possible. Professor Brian Sutton-Smith has been able to describe play, and Mihaly Csikszentmahlyi has been able to describe fun. Stewart Brand's energy and vision led to the development of The New Games Foundation. Pat Farrington brought silliness and sensitivity to The New Games Foundation, and John O'Connell so effectively modeled loving competition. Bill Michaelis continues teaching the spirit of fun, with so much fun, as he has for so many years. Thanks also to the loving, patient, and playful hand of Bob Gregson, whose art, warmth, and whimsy made this book so much more fun.

Introducing
and Implementing
Junkyard Sports

Part one consists of three chapters. The first chapter defines the concept and explores some of the purposes and potential benefits that led to the development of junkyard sports. You will find the first chapter especially useful when you find yourself needing to get permission from parents, faculty, or community sponsors. Sometimes it's hard to put the obvious into words. Chapter 1 will help you do just that.

Chapter 2 examines how a junkyard sport is designed and developed. Specifically, the chapter explains the components of a junkyard sport: people, place, junk, and games. It will also examine the process of game creation.

Chapter 3 develops some ground rules for coaching and facilitating junkyard sports, and gives you a strategy for implementing leadership and for sharing the fun with your peers and students. This chapter, in particular, demonstrates that leading a junkyard sports event is more like coaching than teaching, more like facilitation than coaching, and more fun than either.

CHAPTER 1

Introducing
Junkyard Sports

J unkyard sports are "real" sports and games played with the "wrong" equipment. Because the sports are made up by the people who are playing them, they offer a welcome alternative to the traditional sport programs. Junkyard sports stress personal involvement, active participation by a diverse community, physical and psychological safety, creativity, and most of all, the opportunity to create and share fun.

CONCEPT AND PURPOSE
OF JUNKYARD SPORTS

The concept we're calling *junkyard sports* is as ancient as sport itself. Earlier in the 20th century, this idea was demonstrated on the streets, sidewalks, vacant lots, and backyards of most cities, when games like stickball, box ball, and pie-tin Frisbee could be found virtually everywhere there were kids. Even today, when so many kids spend their precious play time in front of the television or in organized league sports, you'll find kids playing basketball with a trashcan and a paper wad, or playing baseball with a frying pan bat and a ball of rolled-up socks. Playful minds find inspiration in the limitations of equipment, environment, and physical abilities.

Junkyard sports are so inviting because they are based on sports that everyone knows. The inventiveness begins when people play the sports in some unusual place with some wacky piece of equipment that has nothing to do with how the sports are supposed to be played, and then they mix these sports with other sports. This is the spark that ignites the imagination. Junkyard sports are also played with as diverse a group of players as are available—young and old, novices and experts, those with and without disabilities—to create a sport that is truly inclusive. There is no need to adapt a sport for a specific population when the very population that will be playing it is creating it. There is no reason to worry about how willing people will be to play a sport when the sport they are playing is their own.

Junkyard sports are a rich, exciting, and growing resource for physical activities that will work in any environment and with any player. The activities can take anywhere from a half hour to a half day. In five minutes or less you can easily initiate completely new activities for any audience. Kids will use their bodies and minds to develop and exercise their capacity for play, to develop social skills, and to learn from and with each other. They will design and experiment and play as a team.

The process of invention in junkyard sports develops the whole player—body, mind, community, and environment. In the process of developing a new, informal, just-for-fun sport, players combine physical education with cognitive skill development and socialization. From both the educators' and players' perspectives, junkyard sports are invitations to play and opportunities to transcend differences in physical abilities, social status, gender, and age.

There's a big difference between a sport that you learn and a sport that you make up. Sports that you learn, despite their numerous benefits, have a way of separating people. There are those who are good enough, and those who aren't. Sports set the bar, creating a challenge that its players rise to meet. But when you're making up a new sport, the question isn't so much about whether you are good enough to play it. It's about whether the sport is good enough to make you *want* to play. Junkyard sports, then, make it possible for anyone to play with anyone else. As long as they're making up the sport together, they'll find a way to play together. From the perspective of a recreation or youth leader, this makes junkyard sports an ideal vehicle for serving the community. As a class project or as an event, the invention of a new junkyard sport is an opportunity for integration and celebration.

Involvement

There is only one real criterion for measuring the success of a junkyard sports event—involvement. Count the people who are playing and how deeply they are playing. If your star athletes are having the time of their lives and your weaker players are sitting on the sidelines, the design has failed. If your oldest players are dancing with delight and your youngest are hanging back, bored, something's wrong with the event. You might call this a "the more the merrier" principle. And it really works. The more people involved and the more fully they're involved, the better the experience is for everyone.

Complete involvement is a very harsh measure because it's impossible to meet. Even in the best of all sports, and in the best of all junkyards, there'll be times when people just aren't engaged. It's as much part of the nature of play for players to disengage as it is for them to engage. What you hope is that these periods are brief and rare.

Sometimes it's obvious when a game isn't working. It stops being fun. When that happens, above all, don't blame yourself, and don't blame the players. Blame the game. That, after all, is what makes junkyard sports so much fun. The game is only a means to an end. The end is fun—for everyone. You can't force involvement. But you can change the game. You can call a time-out. You can add more junk. You can take away, change, or add a rule or two.

And, of course, while you're changing the game, you're getting everyone involved in the game change. Naturally, during the design session your unrealistic but avowed goal is 100 percent participation.

Diversity

Nothing affects the experience of play as profoundly as the people we are playing with. Their moods, intelligence, abilities, ages, and gender influence what we play and what we think we can play. Bringing together people who don't normally "belong" together to create a new sport that they can all play together is a powerful and humanizing experience for all involved.

It's remarkable how many kinds of people we can bring together with a little applied playfulness. We can play with animals and get so close to them that we and the animals can actually take equal roles in determining the direction and duration of the game. We can play, as equals, with babies and toddlers, with alcoholics and schizophrenics, with people who are blind, and others with a variety of disabilities. Diversity is the name of the game. We bring together diverse materials and environments, diverse games and rules, and a diverse selection of population.

Playfulness is the key. Creating and supporting the willingness to try, to see what happens while we change the rules and materials and environment until everyone who wants to play can play together, equally, are what junkyard sports are for.

Safety

In junkyard sports, one way to ensure safety at every level—physical, social, and emotional—is to make it possible for participants to engage at the level of their own choosing. This way, even if someone feels threatened, she can easily withdraw, regain composure and perspective, and return to the fray in her own good time.

Another way to help create a safe experience is to make and keep things fun. When people laugh a lot, they clearly aren't taking things too seriously. When you hear people laugh together it's a sign that they feel safe and healthy. When animals play, even if we can't recognize their own version of laughter, the same holds true. If they are playing, they feel safe and healthy.

Creativity

Nothing fosters creativity more than a good sense of humor and a willingness to play. Nothing dampens creativity more than a somber, pressured, formal discussion about how to design a game. Get the junk into people's hands as soon as possible. Get them to start playing with the stuff separately, then together. Give them no more than a few suggestions or instructions at a time, like, "Think we can make a baseball game with this stuff?" or "Can we make something we can play on the steps?" As soon as there's a difference of opinion, see if you can get two separate groups going—each focusing on testing out yet another alternative. Help people understand that the only real way to tell whether an idea is a good one is by putting it into practice by playing with it.

Because junkyard sports are played by their inventors, the pressure to perform is shared. Everyone wants the game to succeed. Everyone wants everyone to succeed.

Slanted High Bar Principle

Even when a junkyard sport gets played and refined and players begin to focus more on challenge and performance, and what was more or less a game begins to become a definite sport, you can build fun and safety into the design of the competition by creating challenges that are individually negotiable. In adapted physical education, teachers are given an elegant model, called the *slanted high bar principle,* that puts the concept of individually negotiable challenge into practice.

If you're a physical education teacher, one of the things you do with students is help them develop their high-jumping skills. In "nonadaptive" physical education, you did this by holding jumping contests. You'd hang a horizontal high bar at a certain height and everybody would take a turn jumping over the high bar. If they succeeded, they'd go to the next round, and the high bar was raised. The contest would continue until only one person was left, and that person would be praised as the one who established the high-jump record for the class. A problem with this kind of competitive-incentive structure is that the people who need the most practice are the people who get to jump the least often. The worse they are at jumping, the sooner they're out of the game. Another problem is that no one feels safe. Not even you, the teacher.

Make the high bar diagonal instead of parallel to the ground. Let everybody jump over any part of the high bar, and they can take as many turns as they want. Each kid sets his own challenge. The jumpers who are not so good at jumping can still jump across the high bar as many times as anyone else—they just cross at a lower point. And, when they feel the need to increase the challenge, they can just station themselves at a higher part of the high bar. No one is eliminated. No one is given prizes. Everyone plays at his own level of safety. Everyone wins, repeatedly.

Slant the high bar and the authority rolls right out of your hands—out of any one body's hands, actually—into everybody's hands. The challenge (jump as high as you can, and then jump higher) remains the same, but the challenger has changed. You, the instructor, aren't the one who increases the challenge; the kids create it as a group and individually.

A challenge that is determined by the individual players is more complex because it requires reflective action. The players must evaluate not only their own success but also the success of the challenge. And even though they can get very competitive, the challenge is ultimately self-selected, ultimately guided by sheer fun.

Without an external evaluator, each player can devise and revise the challenge. Of course, evaluation is taking place, and whether the competition is inner directed or outer directed, the jumpers (both higher skilled and lower skilled), and their inner referees are evaluating their performance, challenging them to challenge themselves. Even though nobody's eliminated, even though everyone is free to increase or decrease the challenge, even though they don't even have to take turns, the challenge is directed toward the individual.

Raising the horizontal high bar, you intensify the competitive relationship between the diminishing few. The game, internally and externally, becomes increasingly unsafe. Slant the high bar, and you relax the relationship so that it becomes supportive, empowering, healthy, safe.

SPORTS FOR THE FUN OF IT

One of the most radical of the implications of junkyard sports is the notion that regardless of what gets invented or played or who wins, the only thing that really counts is how much fun it is for everyone. As a criterion for success, especially for those who need to answer to many objectives of educational and public programming, the "fun for everyone" goal can be surprisingly difficult to communicate and defend. Most sport programs are funded by organizations that measure success in terms of the development of very specific athletic competencies—a belief shared by the majority of the people served by these programs. Try telling parents who sent their kids to soccer camp that, although their kids lost almost every game they played and didn't show any particular athletic skill, they succeeded because they had a lot of fun.

The "sports for the fun of it" concept was developed specifically for those people who are not served by sport clubs and competitions—the people for whom participation, and not competition, is the goal. It was developed because we have all begun to recognize that this is a far wider audience, with perhaps even more telling needs than the audiences served by traditional sport programs.

Many of our so-called athletes who excel in sports and eagerly embrace the rigors of traditional physical education and sport programs also ultimately find themselves in a similar position of disenfranchisement and obesity, because they did not achieve or even maintain their star status. Motivated solely by the promise of professional sports, they end up embittered and ill served by the very institutions that had once provided them both purpose and identity.

The "sports for the fun of it" approach subscribes to a very different set of premises. It is based on a faith in human motivation. When people have fun playing, they put more of themselves into play. They engage body, spirit, and mind, challenging themselves to excel because in excellence there is even more fun. When they play, not for score or recognition but for enjoyment, they play for life. Central to the notion of "sports for the fun of it" is the idealistic and often unreachable goal of fun for *all*. As difficult as it may be to achieve, setting this as a goal establishes a focus that is both individually and collectively experienced. It introduces the notion of community and urges the development of both personal and social competencies.

In traditional sports, the game itself determines who is good enough to play. In junkyard sports, the players determine whether the game is good enough. The better the game is, the more fun for the more people for more of the time the game is played. By including players of different ages and abilities, you create an even greater challenge and a more profound accomplishment. The victors of junkyard sports can never be confined to the winning team. Victory is something that happens to the entire community of players and spectators.

By aiming at an experience that is fun for everyone, players have an objective criterion for measuring the success of the game. In the process of attempting to succeed, they also develop social skills that include compassion, communication, acceptance, shared leadership, and shared victory.

CHAPTER 2

Creating a Junkyard Sport

Every junkyard sport has four elements:

1. People
2. Place
3. Junk
4. Games

The more diverse the participants in skill, age, or ability, the more potential for social learning and challenge. For example, a new sport, designed by a group that includes some people who use wheelchairs and some who don't, is a sport that leads to deeper social contact between those groups. Playing with a diverse group makes it impossible to play any known sport without changing the rules, which in turn makes the process of developing junkyard sports so challenging and rewarding. The more specific and unusual the environment, the greater the challenge to players' observation and planning skills.

The more diverse the junk is, the more creative players' reasoning will be. Recommended junk collections include materials for uniforms: foam rubber, tape, bubble wrap, ribbon, along with household objects like brooms, socks, pantyhose . . . the possibilities are endless.

Every junkyard sport is made by combining rules from one sport with those of another game, sport, or toy. Having not just one set of rules, but a collection of rules, makes it possible for participants to adapt the sport more easily to physical, social, and environmental opportunities. The effective selection and combination of rules from two different sports challenges reasoning, creative, and predictive skills.

PEOPLE

Of the four ingredients of junkyard sports, people remain the most important. They have the strongest influence over what gets played and how much fun it turns out to be. There are lots of different ways to classify people. The key word is *different*. The more diverse the mix of people, the more delightful the success of the junkyard sport.

There are a lot of ways to look at the differences among people: ability, age, skill, culture, language, height, strength, gender, alertness, popularity, weight, intelligence, energy. And each combination of people affects the design and experience of a junkyard sport. The greater the diversity, the more unique the challenge to the player and designers.

Coming up with a sport that can be played with equal delight by people with disabilities, seniors, adults, young children, the academically gifted, and cognitively challenged is a gift to all who participate. It creates and extends community. It develops understanding and compassion. It stimulates creativity. Getting people out to play with other populations strengthens their connection to one another and to humanity. The concept of junkyard sports was developed with this in mind. It is often difficult to adapt a traditional sport to the needs of a diverse community. On the other hand, any sport that this community develops for itself is bound to be one that can be played by another community with a similar range of abilities.

PLACE

Here are some of the environments we used in creating the demonstration games: backyard, baseball field, basketball court, beach, cafeteria, curb, dining room, family room, fence, football field, gym, hallway, kitchen, lawn, living room, lunchroom, park, parking lot, playground, shopping mall, sidewalk, skating rink, soccer field, swimming pool, tennis court, wall, woods.

To get a sense of how powerful a factor the environment can become, follow some skateboarders as they turn the world into a skating ramp. Time, weather, and season are also powerful factors, each having its own influence over the nature and success of the junkyard sport event. Your choice of the environment in which the event will be held is almost as important as your selection of people. The wider the range of environments in which people meet to play, the closer the people become as a community and the more varied the junkyard sports they invent. They become closer as a community because as the settings in which they meet change, they get to experience the constancy and uniqueness of each person. Their sports become more varied because they need to adapt not only to changing environments but also to the increased understanding people have of one another's play preferences.

Just getting people out of the environment in which they traditionally meet is often enough to stimulate increased involvement and creativity. The more environments they meet in, the greater the cohesion of the group.

Environment is one of the four variables in the evolution of a junkyard sport. Ask a group to try playing soccer in a swimming pool. It's impossible to follow all the rules. It's just too hard to run or kick in the water. So, they have to find a way to adapt the game, and, in so doing, create a new junkyard sport. Your collection of accessible environments is as powerful a component of your junkmasters' tool kit as the junk you collect.

Finally, your *careful* use of the environment helps players develop a greater sensitivity to their surroundings and responsibilities. When you're playing outdoors, being sure not to litter or trample flowers and being careful to respect property lines and the privacy of nonplayers all contribute to a play experience that is as responsible as it is fun.

JUNK

Junk is definitely the name of the game here. Anything that's official equipment for one sport is another sport's junk. For a football player, a bunch of soccer balls would be considered nothing more than things that need to be put away. For the junkyard football player, that same bunch of soccer balls is an invitation to create at least one, if not 100, new junkyard sports.

If you thumb through part two, "The Junkmasters' Guide," you'll quickly get an idea of the junk we're talking about. The best approach is to take a quick inventory of all the sport equipment you have, as well as supplies like trashcans and brooms and toilet paper. The best junk is the stuff you already have.

On the other hand, once you start playing junkyard sports, you'll definitely look for ways to expand your junk collection. You'll probably borrow stuff like exercise balls or tap shoes or suitcases. You'll even buy new junk. But before you do, you should know about socks and pantyhose. Of all the junk available to you, socks and pantyhose are the funniest and the most versatile. There's something funny about socks. Especially singleton socks. Everybody has them. Nobody knows what to do with them. And we're all a little embarrassed that we have so many. They're so commonplace, and so varied, and even the word sounds funny.

At the same time, socks are marvelous playthings: soft, colorful, safe. Because it's so easy to make a ball out of them, they can be used in hundreds of junkyard sports. And, with a little imagination, they can be used for hundreds more.

Pantyhose are a great addition to any sock collection. They offer the promise of great capacity. How many socks do you think it would take to stuff a pair of pantyhose? It is often said among junkmasters that socks and pantyhose are the nuts and bolts of junkyard sports. Since a good collection of socks and pantyhose is so valuable, you might even consider launching your junkyard sports initiative with a community-wide Clean Used Socks and Pantyhose Drive. It's a great way to involve the community. Many people, for reasons known only to them, keep a collection of unmatched socks and torn pantyhose, hoping against hope to find something useful to do with them. So asking them for contributions is not like asking them to give you money or buy cookies. It's an easy way for them to feel part of your program, and it requires little salesmanship to get them to part with their sock and pantyhose hoard.

Everybody knows how to make a sock ball. You roll a pair of socks together and stretch the top of the sock over the roll. Yet, only a few know that you can make a sock ball out of three socks, or even six—a really good, round, firm sock ball that won't unravel when thrown or kicked or pounced on. Making a good sock ball is a fundamental skill for any true junkyard sportsperson.

The Schmerltz, a throwing toy made from a knee sock and tennis ball, had such wonderfully playworthy properties that it was included in every New Games standard equipment bag. Hold the Schmerltz by the sock end, spin and release, and it takes flight. A well-launched Schmerltz can travel 20 or 30 feet in the air, and while in flight the sock end flutters and flaunts its sockish loveliness for all to see. Obviously, even longer-handled and perhaps more flightworthy Schmerltzes can be made with pantyhose instead of socks. Yes, trees and telephone lines are Schmerltz eaters, so open-field Shmertlzing is always preferred.

You can also hit things with your Schmerltz. In fact, if you hold on to the sock end and whack the ball end into another ball, you have something quite satisfyingly clublike. Not as controllable as a golf club or hockey stick, but masterable, and a lot softer. So, you might want to add old tennis balls to your junk collection.

If you find yourself in the gathering mode, here's a partial list of some of the junk most often used in junkyard sports demonstration games:

backboards	jacks balls	rubber bands
badminton birdies	jingle bells	sandbags
badminton rackets	kickballs	sardine tins
balloons	kneepads	sheets (cloth)
basketballs	knee socks	sheets of paper
beach balls	lacrosse sticks	shoebox lids
beanbags	life preservers	shoes
bedsheets	marbles	shopping carts
blankets	markers	sidewalk chalk
boom boxes	masking tape	silicone juggling balls
broom handles	Masonite	skateboards
brooms	mini sports balls	soccer balls
bubble wrap	mops	soccer goals
buckets	Nerf balls	soda cans
carpet tubes	noisemakers	soup cans
cartons	packing chips	spoons
chairs	paper bags	sponge balls
chalk	paper napkins	sponges
chopsticks	paper plates	squash rackets
cigar boxes	paper-towel tubes	stools
clothesline	parachutes	Super Balls
coins	pencils	tables
crayons	pillowcases	tissues
crepe paper	Ping-Pong balls	toilet paper
cricket bats	Ping-Pong paddles	toilet-paper tubes
croquet mallets	pillowcases	towels
cylinders	place mats	traffic cones
dodgeballs	plastic bowling pins	trashcans
duct tape	plastic buckets	tricycles
egg-shaped balls	plastic cups	tubular webbing
foam rubber	plastic grocery bags	(climbing webbing)
footballs	plastic milk bottles	tuna cans
Frisbees	plastic soda bottles	volleyball nets
goggles	playground balls	water balloons
golf clubs	pool noodles	wheelchairs
gym scooters	punch balls	Wiffle balls
hockey goals	push brooms	Wiffle bats
hockey sticks	PVC pipe	wrist pads
hula hoops	ribbons	yardsticks
index cards	ropes	yarn

Even stuff that's closely identified with a particular sport (such as basketballs, footballs, and tennis rackets) can be the stuff of a new junkyard sport. What makes one sport's equipment another sport's junk is that it's not being used the way it's meant to be used. A football can transform a game of soccer. A tennis ball redefines the experience of baseball.

To develop your sports junkyard, start with the stuff that's easiest to find. Take an inventory of your equipment locker. While you're at it, take an inventory of the janitorial supply closet. And the cafeteria pantry. And the shop. On your way out, take a glance at what's going on near your local trash collector. Between work and home, look for companies that might have some playworthy scraps: carpet stores, computer stores, grocery stores, newspaper offices, packaging stores, shoe stores, clothing and shoe manufacturers, just-about-anything manufacturers. . . . When you get to your neighborhood, ask around. You'll find singleton socks, torn pantyhose, old newspapers, empty plastic milk and soda bottles, rubber bands, bottle caps. . . .

A lot of the junk you collect isn't essential to the play of the sport itself, but it's of great value to the fun of it all—especially the junk that can be used for creating uniforms. That's where junk like bubble wrap and towels, toilet paper and duct tape come in so handy. You can even make costumes for your junkyard cheerleaders and your junkyard marching band (complete with comb-and-tissue-paper kazoos). Uniforms can be minimal (wear the pantyhose on your head) or elaborate (festoon yourself with bubble wrap and duct tape), as suitable for the time and spirit.

Most junkyard sports are unrepeatable, so a video or still camera can be a great boon both to the historians and the players of the junkyard sports community. The presence of a camera can make the game seem more real, more like the kind of sport you see on TV. It can help players focus on their performance and be a source of entertainment and incentive. The people who record the games also have an opportunity for a valuable and much-appreciated role, even though they aren't directly involved in the activity itself.

GAMES

The fourth and equally central component of junkyard sports is the sports and games that are incorporated into its design. In this book, the games are based on six sports: soccer, football, basketball, baseball, hockey, and volleyball. To create such a variety, we combined these sports with each other and with elements of other sports and games: bocce, bowling, box hockey, foosball, golf, marble football, marbles, rugby, pinball, and shuffleboard. Again, the more games the players and designers have to draw on, the greater the variety of the junkyard sport.

Almost every junkyard sport includes rules from some other sport or game. The inspiration for a junkyard sport is drawn from the introduction of some fundamental change in the number or nature of the participants, in the environment within which the sport will be played, or in the equipment that is used. For example, we might try to find a way to play football with 100 people, or in a swimming pool, or with a beach ball instead of a football. Our repertoire of other games and sports makes it possible for us to adapt a sport easily to any of these changes. Any game or sport can become a source for new rules: another sport, a kids' game, even a board game or a paper-and-pencil game. Then there are the basic rule changes that you can make to almost any sport and instantly transform it into an event of junkyard proportions:

Seven Ways to Make Games (and, Actually, Almost Anything) More Fun

1. If there are two sides, add a third or take one away.
2. Every now and then, change sides—when someone is ahead by two somethings or when someone throws a 9, or when somebody has to go to the bathroom.
3. If there are turns (checkers, gin rummy, serving the ball in Ping-Pong or volleyball), take them together, at the same time, as in "1, 2, 3, go," or every now and then skip a turn.
4. If there is a score, keep playing until you discover who's the second winner, and the third, and the next, and the last. Or give each other points, or play pointlessly.
5. If it's not fun, change it: Add another ball, or a rule, or a goal, or take a rule away, or change a rule, or borrow a rule from another game, or add a whole game and play them both at once, or do something silly.

6. If it's still not fun, change yourself. Try it with your eyes closed, or try it with your "wrong" hand, or tie yourself to someone else.

7. If it makes the game better, cheat.

FINDING INSPIRATION

One of the key inspirations for the development of a junkyard sport is playing in the "wrong" environment with the "wrong" equipment. Stickball, for example, was invented so that kids could play baseball on the street. They didn't have bats, so they made them out of sticks. They didn't have gloves, so they used a rubber ball.

Trying to play soccer in a gym is just like trying to play baseball in the street. Certain things just don't work as well—for example, the combined absence of soccer goals with the presence of basketball hoops. It almost begs the question, is it possible to score a basket soccer-style, without using your hands? In theory, definitely, given appropriate kicking and butting skills. In practice, unless you're training a college basketball team, this is a little too much to expect.

Two more variables are who's playing and the junk they're playing with. The more significant of the two variables is who's playing. You have to consider the playing preferences of a wide range of ages and abilities, which is always a good practice when creating a junkyard sport, because junkyard sports are for everybody. Then there's the second variable, the junk. We need a ball, for sure. It could be any kind of ball—soccer ball, basketball . . . well, not a baseball. It could be a balloon or a super ball. Or a beach ball, perhaps. A beach ball has the added advantages of being light and slow, easy to kick and butt, and hard to get hurt by. It also has the disadvantage of being very hard to aim. Generally, you don't have to run a lot to catch up with a beach ball. It'd certainly be a good choice for seniors, for players with limited mobility, and for kids.

Another thing about a beach ball is that it's hard to take seriously. Its lightness gives the game a lightheartedness of its own. So if you use a beach ball, you'd need ways to aim the beach ball, especially if it's supposed to land inside a basketball hoop in order to score (all right, so it can't go through the basket, but it could land in it, and stay there, with a little help).

You could borrow an idea from curling. You could include brooms in your junk pile. Four brooms would be good—two for each team or one for every four players. Brooms can be used to guide the ball into the hoop and knock it out. Depending on how the brooms get used, they could also be a perfect invitation for active participation by people who use wheelchairs.

This is the evolution of the game Beach-Basket Soccer, located on page 36.

CHAPTER 3

Coaching Junkyard Sports

There are five phases in teaching junkyard sports:

1. Playing the demonstration game
2. Inventing a variation
3. Testing
4. Sharing
5. Judging

Your participation as a coach differs from phase to phase.

DEMONSTRATION GAME

During the first phase, the demonstration game, your goal is to introduce the materials and show how they might be used. Notice the emphasis on *might.* The only purpose of the demonstration game activity is to get things started, not to tell people what they're supposed to invent or how they should be using the junk.

Instead of thinking of yourself as a coach, try using the term "junkmaster." All you really need do as junkmaster is collect the junk, decide where you want everyone to meet, and whom you want to invite. In the meantime, the demonstration games in this book get people and ideas moving. They demonstrate that, in fact, given this junk and these people in this place, it is possible to come up with a genuinely playworthy sport. Though the demonstration games described in this book are fun enough to be played for hours, they serve their purpose in 15 minutes or less.

Inventing

In the invention phase, you are junkmaster and facilitator. As junkmaster, you establish the parameters for each of the four elements: the people, the environment, the junk, and the associated game. As facilitator, you institute the decision-making processes that lead to the evolution of a new junkyard sport.

The junkmaster is a role that is central to the experience of junkyard sports. You, someone else, or some group of people should assume responsibility for deciding on where, when, with whom, and with what something gets played. You gather the materials, set the stage, and direct the show.

It's a lot of fun to be junkmaster. You get to challenge people, and yourself, on so many levels. You get to create and lead experiences that engage, entertain, and enlighten. The junkmaster not only decides what junk gets used but also gathers and tests the junk. Using all the junk, engaging all the players, and incorporating as much of the environment as possible, the junkmaster develops her own junkyard sports—demonstration games that are fun enough to get people started on creating their own.

The goal of teaching or leading junkyard sports is achieved when the people who get led or taught then lead and teach their own junkyard sports. You succeed as a teacher of junkyard sports when the people you're playing with become their own junkmasters.

It is generally difficult for people in large groups to invent anything. Most professional facilitators suggest a maximum of eight people per group. This is because the more people that are involved, the more difficult it is for any one person to be heard. The invention of a junkyard sport is a collaborative event, so the easier you can make it for everyone to be involved, the more successful the experience. For this reason, you prepare for a junkyard sport session by establishing a junk pile for each group. There is no rule saying that each group has to have the same materials. If they do, the chances are good that they'll learn from one another's ideas. If they don't, there is a greater opportunity for diversity of sports. The more diverse the groups are in age and ability, the more likely it is that more people will benefit from the sports they create. If it is at all possible, consider inviting people from all sectors of the community to your junkyard sport sessions.

As a rule, the sooner people get actively involved, the more likely it is that they'll stay involved. Conversely, the longer they discuss possibilities, the more likely it is that things will start falling apart. Your main objective, then, is to get them to start playing with the junk, seeing what else they can make it do. As long as they are playing together, they'll have a reliable source of inspiration.

Testing

The testing process begins almost as soon as people start playing with the materials. Once they find something that seems fun to do, the next step is to do it. Once they start doing it, they'll quickly see how they can make it better.

If things go well, there should be no need to get people to stop inventing and start testing their sports. As long as they are playing, it's a seamless process. If some groups have difficulty committing to an idea long enough to play it out, you'll need to remind them about the time limitations.

Focus your coaching skills on the groups that are ready to play. The sooner they start playing, the sooner the other groups will feel the need to commit to something and get started.

Sharing

Now that all the groups have had a chance to develop and test their new junkyard sport, they need to share it with one another. This is the real payoff for many of them—the opportunity to show off and to be entertained by the inventiveness of the other groups. There are two approaches to facilitating this process. The simpler, and more time consuming, is to give each group an opportunity to demonstrate their invention. In an hour-long junkyard sport session, this leaves each group about five minutes—not really enough time for the groups to get more than a taste of each other's inventiveness.

A second approach is the "festival." Have all groups start playing their sports simultaneously. While they're playing, prompt each player to try another game. Establish a "may I cut in" convention: Anyone tapping another player on the shoulder gets to exchange places with that player.

During the festival, emphasize that no one is obligated to play every game or, really, any game. If people want to watch, let them. If they want to wander from game to game, encourage them. This simple permission goes a long way toward creating an environment in which people feel safe to play—physically, emotionally, and socially. If they know they don't have to play, they will tend to play only those sports in which they feel safe. If they feel safe, they will tend to have more fun. If they have more fun, they will be willing to challenge themselves more thoroughly.

Though a bit more difficult to manage, the festival approach tends to make things more, well, festive. No one is in the spotlight. There are no audiences. So the choice of game is more honest. Players can get involved in the sports that interest them the most. There's no pressure to stay within any particular game, so there's a greater sense of choice and playfulness. Also, it helps you and the inventors measure the success of their concepts. The more people who are attracted to their sport (and reluctant to leave), the more likely it is that their sport is one that other people would want to play.

Finally, the festival format can be easily expanded beyond the population of your group. Since there's no longer a need for small-group interaction, other groups, and in fact the entire community, can be invited to participate.

A junkyard sports festival is more like an event than a class. Almost like a theatrical experience. You set the stage, distributing collections of junk around the play area—one for every eight players. You demonstrate a junkyard sport that you've created. Everyone goes into rehearsal, taking your sport, refining it further so that it can be played right there, with whomever they can get, maybe using even more junk. And then the festival happens: all the sports demonstrated and played simultaneously with all the players trying to play each before the festival ends. This approach is dictated as much by sheer logistics as it is by sound pedagogy. It's simply too difficult to keep everyone involved in creating something new if there are more than eight people in a group. If

there are three groups, there'll be three different sports to develop, produce, and play. There's just not enough time.

Playing everything simultaneously lends a festive air and invites people to mix, to play with, and to learn from each other. The festival also gives people a measure of the success of any one design. The more people who choose to play a particular sport, the better. It prepares the participants for producing events on their own for each other and with the community. And it provides everyone with the opportunity to participate, collaborate, invent, test, refine, and develop fun things to do.

Judging

Junkyard sports are self-scoring. The sport that proves most popular during a junkyard sports festival is clearly the winner. The challenges of a junkyard sport are as follows:

- the junk (how much gets used),
- the environment (how much gets used), and
- the players (how many are involved)

The more junk that gets used, the more fully the environment is employed, and the more players involved, the more successful the sport. If you think that it is appropriate to add further incentive or to help your students more objectively assess their success in designing junkyard sports, you can easily assign numerical scores by converting the performance for each challenge to a percentage, and then adding the percentages together as if they were whole numbers. So, a team that used 90 percent of the junk, 65 percent of the environment, and 100 percent of the players would score 255.

In competing against themselves, teams attempt to better their scores at each new junkyard sports festival. In competing against other teams, both teams begin with the same junk and sport connection and compare scores.

In a series of junkyard sports festivals, make every other festival a "players' choice" festival in which players select the sports they've already developed that they want to play again, adding to that team's cumulative score for that particular sport.

JUNKYARD SPORTS COMMUNITY

As the concept of junkyard sports takes hold, a community of junkyard sports players will form around it. Because junkyard sports invite participation across ages and across abilities, this community can grow very large very quickly.

Junkmasters' Guild

The more successful your junkyard sports program, the more likely it is that some of the people in your program will want to carry it forward into their own neighborhoods, acting as junkmasters for friends and family. This is good for everyone because it helps them find ways to play with anyone, anywhere. It's good for their community because it leads to more opportunities to get more people into play. It's good for you because these junior junkmasters become a source of new ideas and fresh energy, allowing you to move from a position of responsibility to one of shared responsibility and freeing you to focus on those who are most in need of your guidance and creativity.

It's to your advantage to encourage this shift in responsibility every way you can. Invite people to talk about their own experiences in creating or facilitating junkyard sports. Invite the most enthusiastic to meet with you after hours to discuss how they might contribute to the expansion of the junkyard sports program. These people become the core group for forming a junkyard sports club. They can become key organizers for your community junk-gathering efforts, co-facilitators during your junkyard sports sessions, and co-coordinators for community junkyard sports festivals.

Going Public

The best way to guarantee the success of your junkyard sports program is to involve as much of the community as you can reach: students and their families, local businesses, neighborhood clubs, and service organizations. One way to involve the greater community is to ask them for things, as in the socks and pantyhose drive described in chapter 2. Another way is to give them something in return, like a couple of exceptional hours of play, creativity, and celebration. This is what we call a community festival. And it's the most logical and best possible evolution of your junkyard sports initiative. It gives everyone who played and invented junkyard sports an opportunity to celebrate and be celebrated. Because they will have to tailor their approach specifically to the event and the players, it gives them further incentive for developing and refining their understanding of junkyard sports.

If you plan on inviting hundreds of participants (and why not?), your junkmasters in training need to develop junkyard sports that lots of different people can play. They have to scour the community for festival-worthy resources. What kinds of scrap are being produced? Is there a carpet store with lots of carpet tubes to get rid of? (You know, those things that carpets get rolled around—giant toilet-paper cores, some of which are 15 or 20 feet long. Just perfect for group javelin throws, or giant pickup sticks, or a really big game of Capture the Flag.) Cardboard cartons? Shoeboxes? Fabric? Newsprint?

Structurally, you follow the same festival format we've already described: many different sports going on simultaneously with players free to go from game to game. The sports and the junk are more varied so that a variety of activities are available— tabletop soccer, beach-ball tennis, sock-ball football. Fill the spaces surrounding the sports events with music and food. Whenever possible, have local community groups supply food (at a modest price) and local artists provide music.

Junkyard Sports League

As festive and engaging as the festival model might be, it is, at best, an occasional celebration of the spirit of junkyard sports. A far more sustainable model for community involvement is Little League, where local teams throughout the community meet regularly to compete for the fun of it.

As in Little League, the focus is on one particular junkyard sport, depending on the season and appropriateness to the community. The public gets invited to a weekly game of junkyard baseball, or junkyard golf, or maybe junkyard track and field.

The key, of course, is junk. The sport is presented with all the junk-like trappings you can accumulate: uniforms (made, of course, by the players, out of junk), junk sports equipment, teams of intergenerational cheerleaders wearing towels and sheets for costumes, marching and wheelchair bands playing comb-and-tissue-paper kazoos.

Fans sit in an assortment of beach and folding chairs, boxes and blankets. Junk-clad mascots encourage laughter and participation. People with placards form a living scoreboard. Maybe you can even find a karaoke boom box for the team of sports commentators. Vendors hawk five varieties of peanut-butter celery sticks. With much fanfare, the junkmasters (the winners of a previous game) present a new, never-been-played junkyard sport of their own devising. The teams, each a diverse group of playful players, then compete against each other for the fabled Styrofoam Junkmasters' Cup and the opportunity to be junkmasters for the next game.

With the right people and junk, any sport can be made into a junkyard sport worthy of beholding: junkyard football, junkyard basketball, junkyard track and field, even junkyard Olympics, with slanted hurdles and high jumps and poles to vault.

Once you've set your junkyard sports league into motion, invite the press and local authorities. Invite them into every part of the event and event preparation. Get them all to play together, and the future of your junkyard sports program will be virtually and materially assured.

PART TWO

The Junk masters' Guide

P art two is the "Junkmasters' Guide" with six chapters devoted to junkyard versions of soccer, football, basketball, baseball, hockey, and volleyball. Each chapter includes demonstration games for many different environments ranging from the gym, playground, and classroom to the hallway, street, backyard, swimming pool, and even living room. The goal is to provide you with tools that will help students and associates practice the junkyard method wherever they are. Creating a junkyard sport develops social, creative, and reasoning skills, the benefits of which extend well beyond the practice of sports.

Any of the demonstration games can become the inspiration for a new junkyard sport. For example, when looking in the baseball section, you might come across a demonstration game for a version of baseball that can be played in a gym. You might see an idea for a baseball-like sport played with a towel for a bat, a paper wad for a ball, coffee cans for bases, and the batter sitting on an exercise ball. In the next demonstration game, everyone in the field might be carrying a lacrosse stick, and there are two batters, both holding on to either end of a towel. In another, a few people play Box Ball with a ball, the sidewalk, and a piece of chalk.

Using a demonstration game, or a combination of demonstration games, you can get people started on creating their own, invented-on-the-spot junkyard sport. That sport in turn becomes the demonstration game for yet another group, and the invention of yet another unique junkyard sport.

Most junkyard sports, even the best of them, get played at least once before they are replaced by some other, even more fun junkyard sport. And even then, they rarely get played the way they were designed to be played. Often, before the game gets started, somebody discovers a last-minute "wouldn't it be even more fun" idea—which, of course, is exactly what we want to have happen. We want the people who are playing the game to own the game, to think of it as something they created, specifically for each other, for the time and space and the junk they had to play with. That way, the game never gets too important. The focus can stay on the fun of it all—of creativity and spontaneity, of inclusion and safety, of exercising body and mind, heart and soul.

CHAPTER 4

Junkyard Soccer

S occer is one of the most popular of all sports. It draws participation from almost all nationalities, from men and women,
girls and boys. For that reason, this is the first sport we'll be
playing with.

As you page through this collection of soccer demonstration
games, and all the demonstration games that follow (football,
basketball, baseball, hockey, volleyball), remember that each
demonstration game is itself a collection of ideas for making
other demonstration games. Think about the people you'll be
playing with, the space they'll be playing in, and the equipment
and miscellaneous junk you can make available to them. Even
if you don't have the exact materials described in a particular
demonstration game, it's a start.

Marbles Soccer

A combination of marbles and soccer in which players move a larger target ball toward the goal by kicking smaller balls into it.

Starting at opposite ends of the field, players race to kick any ball into the large ball, trying to get the large ball to cross the opposing side's goal line. A team scores 1 point when the bigger ball crosses the opposing team's goal line. The team with the most goals at the end of 20 minutes wins. It is illegal to kick the large ball. Any ball that crosses a boundary line is out of play.

▶PLAYERS

Two teams of 3 to 30 players per team, depending on how much space you have to play.

▶SPACE

This game can be played in any open space: a soccer field, playground, gym, open field, hallway, or protected alley. You'll need boundary lines on all sides of a rectangular field, with a goal area on each end. Normal soccer field dimensions are 50 by 100 yards. Goals are set in the middle of either end of the field and are usually around 8 yards wide.

▶JUNK

The game requires at least one larger ball and a lot of smaller balls (at least one per player). The smaller balls need to be large enough to kick. The larger ball needs to be light enough so that it will move some distance when hit by a smaller ball. The balls can be made out of socks. If you can't find enough socks, try tennis balls. The larger ball can be a playground ball, a beach ball, or even a balloon.

▶SETUP

- Give each team an equal number of smaller balls. Place the larger ball in the middle of the field.
- Both teams line up at opposite goal lines and start kicking and running at the same time.
- One or more players on each team can be designated as goalies.

▶SAFETY

Encourage players to kick the small balls so that they roll on the ground. There should be no physical contact between players. Players who have

difficulty running should be stationed near the periphery of the field where they can help redirect balls back into play.

▶ COACHING TIPS

- If you see ball herding or hoarding, encourage players to examine strategic trade-offs. For example, if they're hoarding, they're not moving the ball.

- Encourage players to pass any extra balls to teammates who need them.

- If the majority of the group has difficulty running, play on a shorter, narrower field. Players stay in position near the goal line, kicking the balls toward the target ball, but without running.

- If it's too difficult to score a goal in the allotted time, consider adding more target balls.

Slip-and-Crawl Soccer

Imagine players on their hands and knees, scooting backward,
with socks.

Teams score by getting the ball to cross the line marking the opponent's end of the court. The winning team scores more goals in the allotted time (20 minutes). The ball can only be kicked or butted. No physical contact between players.

▶PLAYERS

Two teams of 3 to 20 players per team. Depending on the size of the space, there should be no more players per team than can stand shoulder to shoulder along the goal line.

▶SPACE

Any room with a slippery floor: a gym, cafeteria, hallway, or shopping mall.

▶JUNK

With enough socks, you can make balls and elbow pads and kneepads. You can also make balls and padding out of socks, pantyhose, and towels. The ball can be a soccer ball, basketball, playground ball, beach ball, or even a balloon. (The larger and lighter the ball, the gentler the play.)

▶SETUP

- Players take off their shoes.
- They wrap elbows, feet, and knees; get on their hands and knees; and crawl and slide backward across the gym floor, staying on their hands and at least one knee while using the other leg to kick the ball.
- If players are on a basketball court, the lines are clearly marked. Anywhere else, use shoes to mark the boundary. A junior high basketball court is 74 feet long and 42 feet wide. You could play on just a quarter of it and still have fun.
- Goalies kneel within the free-throw zone and can only use the hands or the head to deflect the ball.

▶SAFETY

Encourage sliding backward on all fours only. Discourage anything similar to moving headfirst or getting up and getting a running start. High kicks are always dangerous. Remind the players to keep their heads down.

▶COACHING TIPS

- Passing the ball from player to player is a difficult challenge when crawling or sliding backward, but it's a fun one!
- Have players experiment with sliding—pushing themselves along with their hands while keeping their knees still.
- For more involvement, add more balls.

Beach-Basket Soccer

A soccer version of basketball with a very light ball.

Earn 2 points by getting the beach ball to land in the opposing team's basket. The team with more points by the end of the timed round (20 minutes) wins. Broomies (who act as goalies, but with brooms) must use both brooms. Players may not cross the free-throw line. The beach ball must stay in the hoop, untouched, for at least 5 seconds for the goal to count.

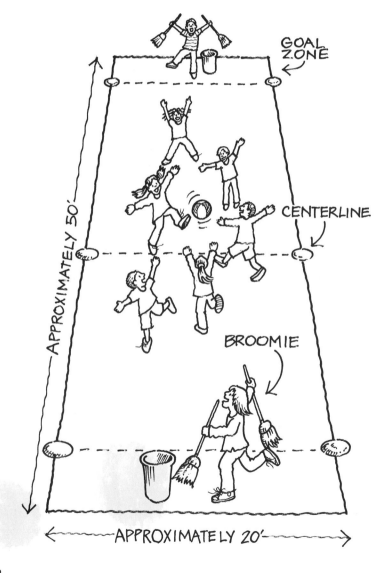

GOAL ZONE

CENTERLINE

BROOMIE

APPROXIMATELY 50'

APPROXIMATELY 20'

▶ PLAYERS

Two teams of 3 to 20 players per team. Players with limited mobility can be broomies.

▶ SPACE

A gym or playground with a basketball court. Or you can use any open space, approximately 20 feet wide and 50 feet long, with boxes or trash-cans on either end functioning as goals. You'll need to mark out a centerline and boundaries around the perimeter and goal zone (basket).

▶ JUNK

All you need is a beach ball and four brooms. Instead of a beach ball, you can try something lighter, like a balloon, or heavier, like a playground ball, dodgeball, or kickball. Instead of brooms, you can use mops, yardsticks, or just broom handles.

▶ SETUP

- Two players are named broomies, and each is positioned at either end of the court. Each has two brooms. The brooms will be used to get the ball to stay in the basket. (These players act as goalies, but instead of trying to keep the ball out of the goal, they are actually trying to keep it in the goal.)
- Players begin the game in center court, with the teams facing each other.
- The ball is tossed in between them, and the first team to kick or butt the ball gains possession.

▶ SAFETY

Players may not touch each other. Players should practice maintaining adequate distance from the broomie.

▶ COACHING TIPS

- Getting hit by a broom is a foul. And that's that. New broomie!
- If it's taking too long to score, try playing with more beach balls, baskets, and brooms.

Kick-Bowl Soccer

Soccer with bowling pins for a goal.

As in soccer, each team tries to kick the ball into the opposing goal. The score of the goal depends on how many tubes get knocked over. The higher-scoring team after the elapsed time (20 minutes) wins, or the first team to get a strike wins. Players can only kick or butt the ball. There are no goalies. The game starts in the middle of the field with players lined up on either side of the centerline. The score is determined by how many pins are knocked over. (For example, if 5 pins are knocked over that team scores 5 points.)

▶PLAYERS

Two teams of one to eight people per team.

▶SPACE

This game can be played almost anywhere. A hallway is probably the best place—a space approximately 10 feet wide and 30 feet long. Wider and longer is also good—up to the dimensions of a soccer field (50 yards by 100 yards). If the space is too wide, use boundary markers for the right and left sides. No goal markers are needed.

▶JUNK

You need a ball that is good for kicking (a soccer ball, kickball, volleyball, or sock ball) and 20 toilet-paper tubes, or lightweight bowling pins, or anything that can be bowled over.

▶SETUP

Place bowling-pin array of toilet-paper tubes at each goal.

▶SAFETY

Keep the ball low so that it doesn't cause any injuries. If this becomes a problem, use a sock ball or foam ball.

▶COACHING TIPS

- If players score too easily, add goalies.
- If it gets crowded, station players in zones, as in foosball. Do the same if the population is diverse in capabilities.

Volley Soccer

Play volleyball and soccer at the same time.

Teams serve simultaneously. The soccer ball can only be kicked under the net; the volleyball can only be volleyed over the net. Players cannot touch the soccer ball with their hands, nor can they touch the volleyball with their feet.

The team that serves the soccer ball earns 1 point every time the soccer ball crosses the back boundary of the volleyball court. The team that serves the volleyball receives 1 point every time the volleyball is not legally returned. If one player on either team simultaneously returns both balls, that team receives an extra point. Both teams observe the volleyball convention that limits each team to three hits of the ball before it must get to the other side of the net, and no one player can hit either ball in succession. The team with more points at the end of 20 minutes wins.

▶PLAYERS

Two teams of 2 to 15 players per team.

▶SPACE

A tennis or volleyball court, backyard, or playground with anything that you can stretch a net or clothesline across. A regulation volleyball court is about 30 by 60 feet.

▶JUNK

Two balls (a soccer ball and a volleyball), or a beach ball, large exercise ball, egg-shaped ball, cylinder-shaped ball, balloons . . . any kind of ball that's bigger than a softball.

▶SETUP

- Two teams on either side of the court, separated by a net.
- One team has a volleyball, and the other team has a soccer ball, but all players on both teams will play with both balls.

▶SAFETY

Since there are two different balls going in two different directions, one traveling in the air and the other on the ground, it's best to use soft balls, especially when first trying the game. A soft volleyball, or even a beach ball, and a soft soccer ball or sock ball are best. Play a few warm-up rounds before starting the "real" game. Start with as few as three players per side so that teams can begin to understand and anticipate safety issues. Make sure that any player is empowered to stop the game to address safety concerns.

▶ *COACHING TIPS*

- Since the soccer ball travels on the ground and players are facing the opposite team, kickers need to be careful to avoid hitting other players.
- Encourage passing.
- Try playing this game cooperatively, with the goal being to see how many balls can be kept in motion.
- If people want to keep score, have everyone shout out "Goal!" when a soccer goal is made. This will help keep the count and add to the fun.

Play golf with a soccer ball on a course that you create one hole at a time.

Players or teams keep score individually, and 1 point is tallied for each kick. As in golf, the player or team with the lowest score at the end of the course wins. The group decides on the location of the next "hole" and estimates par. Each player kicks the ball when it's his or her turn. The next player kicks the ball from where it landed as a result of the previous kick. Teams alternate players until the target is hit. Each team plays as an individual, sharing the score.

▶ PLAYERS

Two to six individual players; up to four players playing as teams.

▶ SPACE

Play almost anywhere—on a path through the woods, a sidewalk, playground, hallways.

▶ JUNK

You need a kickable ball for each team or player. A mini sports ball (about 4 inches in diameter) to a full-size soccer ball, kickball, or volleyball will work.

▶ SETUP

- Players get into teams. Each team gets one ball.
- The whole group (all players) determines location of the first "hole" (target) and estimates par (how many kicks it will take to kick the ball to the target).

▶ SAFETY

- Players who are waiting their turn should stand behind the kicker. If there are players ahead, the kicker should shout "Fore!" before kicking.
- If players are going in groups, wait until one group has finished the hole before the next group starts.

▶COACHING TIPS

- To add fun and make the challenge more even, pair weaker and stronger players together and have them try to kick simultaneously.
- For the fun of it, encourage the use of golf terminology.
- Encourage players to estimate par accurately.
- You can play with anything that's safely kickable. A soccer ball might prove too dangerous if the area is crowded, and a beach ball will be too difficult to control, especially if it's windy.
- You can play competitively or cooperatively. To play competitively, each player would need a ball. To play cooperatively, both teams share the ball. The kick rotates between players until every player has a turn, and the score is the total number of kicks it takes to reach the goal.

Racketless Racquetball Soccer

Soccer played against a wall, using racquetball rules.

Teams (one to four players) take turns. The serving team kicks or butts the ball against the wall. The receiving team tries to hit the ball back into the wall before it has hit the floor twice or crosses a boundary line. If the ball crosses the back boundary line, or bounces more than two times, the team that kicked it last scores a point. Unlike volleyball, there is no separation between teams, and players move freely across the court. As in volleyball, only the serving team scores. If the receiving team misses, the serving team continues. If the serving team misses, the receiving team serves for the next round. The team with the higher score at the end of the time limit (20 minutes) wins.

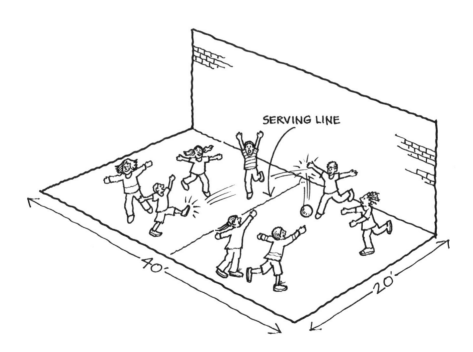

▶PLAYERS

Two teams of one to four players each.

▶SPACE

- You need at least one wall about 20 feet wide or wider. You also need a space that is about 40 feet deep.
- Left and right boundaries are 20 feet apart. Rear boundary is 40 feet in front of the wall.
- If playing inside, include the left and right walls in play.
- Draw a serving line near the middle of the court.

▶JUNK

One or more balls at least 4 inches in diameter (soccer balls, kickballs, even beach balls).

▶SETUP

- Players stand in line facing a long, high wall.
- Boundary lines can be drawn with chalk as described previously.

▶SAFETY

Caution players to keep the ball low and to keep their eyes on it at all times.

▶COACHING TIPS

- Team size, the number of balls in play, the length of the intervals between the adding of more balls, and the distance to the boundary line are all variables that increase or decrease the difficulty of the challenge.
- To increase participation (and decrease competition), add another ball every time a goal is scored.
- To increase the challenge, start with more balls, include a variety of balls, or decrease the distance to the boundary line.
- Allow the teams to decide how many balls they want to start with.

Bocce-Box Soccer

Bocce with objects that you kick instead of roll.

As in bocce, the goal is to get your objects (boxes) closer to the target objects than your opponents' boxes get to the objects. Whoever has more objects closer to the target object at the end of the round wins. Follow traditional bocce or horseshoe rules. Play in two or more teams, each team or player having a unique set of bocce boxes. Players take turns, rotating within teams. Teams take turns, one shot per team. The game is scored after the last box is kicked.

▶ *PLAYERS*

Two to six individual players per team, up to six teams.

▶ *SPACE*

Sidewalks, hallways, shopping malls, and other enclosed walkways at least 6 feet wide and 20 feet long.

▶ *JUNK*

You'll need one smaller box to act as the target ball and four similarly colored, larger boxes for each team. The four larger boxes need to be large enough to be kicked. Covering them with socks will help them slide and will also help if they are not already a similar color.

▶ *SETUP*

One player starts the game by kicking the target object as far down the sidewalk as possible.

▶ *SAFETY*

Be aware of traffic. If a box goes off the edges of the sidewalk, pick it up by hand and put it back into play.

▶ *COACHING TIPS*

- Flat sliding things don't go into the street as easily as round rolling things, which is why they are recommended for playing on a sidewalk.
- The game can be played with balls in a safe environment. Consider using sock balls or small round balls.
- If the challenge isn't high enough, allow the target-box kicker two or more kicks before the round starts.

Hopping Soccer

Soccer played on an extended hopscotch court.

The goal is to kick the "potsie" (the traditional name for the stone used in a game of hopscotch) into the opponent's goal zone. The team with more goals at the end of 20 minutes wins. Teams begin in their goal zones and race to the center to be the first to kick the potsie.

While hopping on one foot, players try to kick the potsie into their opponent's goal.

Players who step on a line or touch the ground with their free foot must go back to their goal zone and begin again. Players may not touch other players with any parts of their bodies.

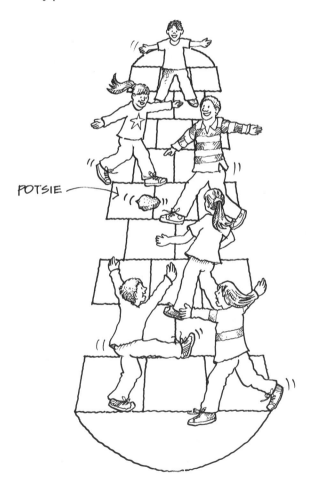

POTSIE

▶ PLAYERS

Two teams of two to nine players per team.

▶ SPACE

Playground, driveway, or any place you can draw on with chalk.

▶ JUNK

Sidewalk chalk and a potsie. The potsie can be made out of a sock ball or beanbag or small box or anything that's easy to kick and won't roll too far. Masking tape to mark boundary lines is all you need to make this an indoor game.

▶ SETUP

- Draw a hopscotch court that is at least three squares wide (if only two players on a team), or up to nine squares wide (as wide as the number of players on a team).
- A square should be wide enough for a player to stand in.
- The court should be an uneven number of squares wide and at least nine rows long.
- Draw a semicircular goal zone on either end.
- Place the potsie in the center square.

▶ SAFETY

Suggest that players always hold one foot in one hand. This will help them focus on hopping.

▶ COACHING TIPS

- If it's too challenging to play as described, allow players to stand on both feet before kicking. If it's not challenging enough, start with two potsies.
- For variation and strategic interest, give some squares a special function: both feet, hand and foot, turn around, and so on.

4.10 Blind Robot Soccer

A soccer game in which players can't move themselves.

Each team has one or more "movers." Movers move simultaneously. A moved player can take no more than one step. One or more soccer balls are in play. There are no goalies. Score by kicking the ball over the opponent's goal. The team scoring more goals in the 20-minute time period wins.

PLAYERS

Two teams of 6 to 25 players per team.

SPACE

Can be played on a soccer field or any open space, indoors or out, approximately 50 feet by 100 feet. Goal zones and boundaries need to be marked.

JUNK

One or more soft soccer balls (partially deflated, or foam) or sock balls or beach balls. Use blindfolds (paper bags are good) for each player.

SETUP

- Once players assume positions on the soccer field, they may not move unless moved by a mover, though they can kick at any time.
- Teams appoint one mover for every three players.
- The mover directs the players by holding the player at the waist and gently turning and moving them into position.

SAFETY

- There's no running, so this greatly minimizes safety concerns for those with mobility or sight impairments. Reduce the number of movers if too much movement becomes a concern.
- Use a soft ball to reduce the shock if it hits a sight-impaired player.

COACHING TIPS

- Increase the number of movers to increase engagement. Ideally, there are enough movers to keep all the remaining players in motion, and there are enough players to kick the ball.
- If things get slow, consider using a mix of balls of different sizes.

Pinball Soccer

A human pinball machine.

Create a human pinball machine with players acting as "shooters," "kickers," "bumpers," and "flippers." The goal of the shooter is to get the highest cumulative score. The rest of the players act as pinball machine parts. Players who are part of the "pin" (those round things that light up, kick the ball, and score) keep the score. Each time they kick the ball, they announce the cumulative score (which can be an additional point, or 10 points, or 100 points, and so on). If you can kick, you can play Pinball Soccer. There's no running.

▶**PLAYERS**

There aren't any teams, and you can play with any number from 6 to 60.

▶**SPACE**

Any fairly open space—a classroom, cafeteria, lawn, playground, or park. Figure at least 8 feet by 20 feet.

▶**JUNK**

You'll need a push broom, tables, chairs, and something kickable to act as pin balls: sock balls, playground balls, volleyballs, beach balls, or balloons. The ball choice depends on the fragility of the space you're playing in and the people you're playing with.

The broom is used as a plunger—the mechanism that starts the ball rolling. You can also use a mop or even a golf club or croquet mallet. Or, the player who shoots can kick or even roll it into play.

▶SETUP

- Position chairs, back to back, in circles of three or more, to be the pins. People sit in those chairs and kick the ball when they can.
- Position other chairs in rows to serve as the bumpers so that they can kick a ball to someone in a pin.
- Place tables by the shooter's position and around the periphery for the ball to go through (ending the turn).
- Create a corridor for the ball ramp. Use a push broom for a plunger.

▶SAFETY

Don't try this with a real soccer ball unless you're in a damage-proof area. The ball can still get lofted, so encourage players to use their heads as well as their feet.

▶COACHING TIPS

- If the ball is escaping too easily, station people to sit on the tables as well and kick the ball back into play.
- Adjust the width of areas where the ball can escape so that most shots last at least two minutes.
- Encourage players to get into the fantasy. Add new sounds, bumpers, kickers, and scoring possibilities. Consider special bumpers that release extra balls.
- Try it with two shooters at a time, both pushing the broom together. They also could play as flippers after the launch.

Foosball Soccer

Human foosball.

A goal is scored when the ball crosses into the goal zone of the opposing team. The team with more goals at the end of the period (20 minutes) wins. Players must always keep one foot on their line.

When players are ready to begin, a ball is started down the 10-yard lines on both sides of the field and kicked down the field.

▶PLAYERS

Two teams of 15 to 50 players per team.

▶SPACE

Football field, sidewalk, parking lot, or any open area that has regular demarcations.

▶JUNK

Two soft or slightly deflated soccer balls, more balls, different kinds of balls (Wiffle balls, beach balls, exercise balls).

▶SETUP

- Players position themselves on the lines of a football field.
- Team members stand on every other line, as in foosball.

▶SAFETY

There is very little physical contact between players. The only "dangerous" object is the ball. That's why a padded (Nerf) ball is suggested.

▶COACHING TIPS

- Players of a wide range of ages and abilities can play this game.
- Consider having the class play foosball before this session.

Three-Team Soccer

Soccer played with three teams.

Keep balls from crossing your team's goal line. The team that scores gets a point for every goal. The team with the higher score at the end of the period (20 minutes) decides the next game. As in soccer, players can't touch the ball with their hands. There is no physical contact between players.

▶PLAYERS

Three teams of 3 to 11 players per team.

▶SPACE

Soccer field with three soccer goals in a Y formation. This game can be played in any open space. Use found or included objects to create goals when necessary.

▶JUNK

At least two soccer balls and three soccer goals. You can add more soccer balls and other kinds of balls.

▶SETUP

- Three soccer goals arranged in a Y formation
- Three teams
- Two soccer balls

▶SAFETY

The more balls in play, the more fun, but also the more difficult it is to monitor individual safety. Consider adding more referees and officials.

▶COACHING TIPS

- Usually the easiest way to score is by forming a temporary coalition with another team. The best defense then becomes offense.
- If teams score too easily, consider assigning players to be goalies. Be sure that goalies are appropriately outfitted (wrapped in layers of foam or bubble wrap) to prevent injury.
- If it takes too long for a team to score, consider adding more balls.

CHAPTER 5

Junkyard Football

Tackling, like any kind of rough-and-tumble play, can definitely be fun. On the other hand, since we'll be in the process of inventing new junkyard sports, it is unlikely that all the necessary safety precautions that keep tackling fun will be in place. For this reason, none of the junkyard football demonstration games described in this chapter includes tackling. Fortunately for the junkyard spirit, at least two variations of football don't require tackling: flag football and touch football. We'll take every advantage of those variations. And, for the fun of it, we'll follow the applicable rules of official football . . . unless they're not fun enough. There are many alternatives to tackling. The ideas in this chapter will start people inventing more than a few.

One of the fun things about sports like football and hockey is the uniform. There's so much padding and color that it's almost impossible to think of playing any junkyard variation without including some kind of junkyard version of costumes. This adds a wonderful element of fun and, well, silliness. Making uniforms out of toilet paper, bubble wrap, towels, masking tape, socks, ribbon, packing chips, and pantyhose adds greatly to the creativity and humor of the experience. On the other hand, no handmade uniform can protect players from injury as well as the official equipment. Yes, you can make shoulder pads out of bubble wrap. But you certainly wouldn't want to rely on them.

When you start creating your junkyard sports, you should definitely consider setting aside 15 minutes and a lot of interesting junk for the creation of uniforms. But be careful to keep it all in the context of fun rather than protection from injury.

Viking Soccer Football

A soccer game with football strategy.

All players wear hats. Throughout the game, players should try to take one another's hats, because a player whose hat has been taken cannot run for the duration of the play. Hatless players may kick the ball and they can try to remove another player's hat if the ball or the other player is close enough. Players cannot touch one another or their own hats, and they cannot touch the ball with their hands. They can only kick the ball. If the ball is kicked out of play (crossing the boundary line), the play ends. The team that kicked the ball out of play loses possession. The next play begins along the yard-line marking where the ball was kicked out of play. Before the play begins, hatless players retrieve their hats.

The team that kicks the ball into the opponent's goal scores 6 points. The team with more points after 20 minutes of play wins. If there's no score, the team closer to the opponent's end zone wins.

▶*PLAYERS*

Two teams of 3 to 15 players per team.

▶*SPACE*

- A regulation football field measures 360 feet from goalpost to goalpost and is 160 feet wide. Each goal is in the center of either end of the field

LET THE GAMES BEGIN.

and is 40 feet wide. Football can, however, be played on almost any open space, from beach to backyard.

- Soccer football can be played on a regulation field or on a field a quarter of the size. You'll need boundary markers on the right and left sides of the field and something to mark the goals.

JUNK

- Viking caps for each player. These can be made out of pantyhose and sock balls. The sock balls (a different color for each team) are placed in the toe of each leg of a pair of pantyhose. The toe is then knotted so that the balls are secure. The players fit the opening of the pantyhose over their heads so that the balls hang down on either side of the head like Viking braids.
- If you want to make uniforms, collect a variety of scrap materials, padding, and tape.
- Anything kickable can serve as a ball—a football, a rolled-up towel stuffed inside a pair of pantyhose, a beach ball. Use four whistles or noisemakers, one for each referee.

SETUP

- Divide players into two teams.
- Select two referees from each team.
- Teams begin at either end of the field at the equivalent of the 20-yard line.
- One team is in possession of the ball and begins the game by kicking it toward the other team.
- As soon as the ball is kicked, both teams begin running toward the ball.

SAFETY

Emphasize that no physical contact is allowed. Be sure that "uniforms" are secure and won't interfere with running. Be sure that hats are not pulled down below the forehead or ears so that they can be easily removed without hurting anyone.

COACHING TIPS

To keep as many people as possible in play, make it a rule that players who touch other players or violate another rule exchange places with a referee.

Schmerltz Football

A game of catching, running, and passing.

The team in possession of the ball flings the ball downfield. The football can be thrown or it can be flung by its pantyhose tail. Players run toward each other. If the opposing team retrieves the ball, players position themselves to receive or block the next pass.

Any player who runs with the football or touches another player trades places with a referee. A team scores 6 points by completing a pass in the opponent's end zone (touchdown). The team that scores more points at the end of 20 minutes wins. If there's no score, the team closer to the opponent's end zone wins. No running with the football is allowed.

▶ PLAYERS

Two teams of 4 to 15 players per team.

▶ SPACE

Football field, soccer field, or any open play space at least 20 feet wide and 60 feet long, with clearly marked boundaries on all sides.

▶ JUNK

- A football (or a foam football or a large sock ball) tied into a pair of pantyhose so that there is a long handle
- Boundary markers (e.g., socks, shoes, anchored rope, or ribbon)
- Whistles or noisemakers for the referees

▶ SETUP

- Group divides into two teams.
- Each team selects a referee.
- Both teams begin the game at opposite ends of the field, around the 20-yard line.

▶*SAFETY*

- Because there's almost constant running in this game, consider calling halftime after 10 minutes if people seem fatigued.

- Do not allow any movement after the whistle is blown, until the penalty is resolved.

▶*COACHING TIPS*

- Encourage players to add other football elements—field goals or defensive safety and corner positions.

- As a warm-up, have players toss the football back and forth, twirling it by the handle and then releasing it.

- Consider giving extra points for a touchdown when a player catches the football by the tail.

Scrum Football

One circle equals one scrum equals one player.

Each scrum acts as a football player. The ball or balloon is moved by kick-passing from scrum to scrum. There is no tackling but much pushing and passing. When scrums collide, they can try to push each other out of bounds in what is known as the interscrum push-off. The goal is to get the football into the opponent's end zone. The team with the higher score at the end of 20 minutes wins. If there's no score, the team closer to the opponent's end zone wins. Standard football scoring applies: 6 points for a touchdown (carrying the ball across the goal), 3 points for a field goal (kicking a ball from the field over the goalposts), 2 points for a safety (pushing a scrum out of bounds behind their own goal line), and 1 extra point for a successful kick over the goalposts after a touchdown.

▶ PLAYERS

There are two teams. Each team forms scrums (groups within the team) of three to eight players. You will have several scrums per team. Since each scrum acts as a single player, you can play the game with 6 to 66 players per team.

SPACE

- An open play area, indoors or out, at least 15 feet wide and 30 feet deep.
- Boundaries should be marked on all sides of the playing area. Goal zones are at either end.
- The game can be played in a swimming pool or backyard, playground or gym, football field or beach.

JUNK

Anything kickable: a football, soccer ball, beach ball, balloon. It is a good idea to start with a balloon, because it helps the players take the game more lightly (forgive the pun). A balloon is more difficult to control, easier to loft in the air, and responsive to the slightest kick. As players' competencies increase, different kinds of balls can be introduced. Bring lots of spare balloons or kickable balls. For fun, try a larger exercise ball or a smaller, mini-soccer ball.

SETUP

Teams form scrums. A scrum is at least three players with their arms around one another's shoulders.

SAFETY

- Teams should practice intrascrum (passing the ball from player to player within a scrum) and interscrum (passing the ball from scrum to scrum) kick-passing, as well as interscrum pushing off.
- Wheelchairs, walkers, canes, and prosthetics can be used only by their owners.

COACHING TIPS

- Blow up the balloons equally and fully.
- Keep scrums tightly formed to avoid scrum-to-scrum kicking or intra-scrum injury.
- Consider trying the game with a "scrum captain," someone who stands in the middle of each scrum to guide it.

Spoon Football

Tackle someone by knocking the object out of his spoon.

Each player has a soup spoon and a sock ball. Players can move only if the sock ball is in their spoon. It is illegal to touch the sock ball with anything other than the spoon. If a player drops the object, she must stop and retrieve it before continuing. Players may pick up their spoons. Players may knock the sock ball off of the opposing players' spoons. The goal is to carry the football into the opponent's end zone. Score 6 points for a touchdown. The team with the higher score at the end of 20 minutes wins. If there's no score, the team closer to the opponent's end zone wins. There is no tackling.

▶PLAYERS

Two teams of 5 to 11 players per team.

▶SPACE

Football or soccer field, playground, gym, or park.

▶JUNK

A soup spoon and sock ball for each player, a football, and boundary markers if players are not on a football or soccer field. If necessary or for fun, substitute soda straws for spoons; substitute small sponge balls for socks; substitute plastic glasses and water for spoons and socks; substitute a six-sock sock ball or a soccer ball for a football.

▶SETUP

- Players start at opposite ends of the field.
- The team in possession of the ball kicks off.

▶SAFETY

Emphasize that the spoons are to be used only for picking up and carrying the sock ball.

▶COACHING TIPS

- Practice running with spoons before starting the game.
- Try playing in slow motion first; this will help players get a feel for the added challenge.

Poison-Sock Football

Football with a bit of freeze tag and dodgeball thrown in.

A team scores a touchdown (6 points) by carrying the ball into the opponent's end zone. The team with the higher score at the end of 20 minutes wins. If there's no score, the team closer to the opponent's end zone wins. Any player on offense who is hit by a sock ball is "tackled" and must fall down. If the player carrying the football is hit by a sock ball, the play is over. The next play resumes from that position (scrimmage line) on the field.

No physical contact is allowed. Thrown sock balls cannot be retrieved during that play.

▶PLAYERS

Two teams of 3 to 15 players per team.

▶SPACE

- Any open space—football field, beach, playground, gym—at least 15 by 30 feet. The smaller the space is, the more difficult the game will be for the offensive team.
- Boundaries and goal areas are marked. The goal areas are in the middle of either end zone, approximately the width of the playing area.

▶JUNK

- A football or a foam football, soccer ball, or kickball
- Boundaries made out of socks, shoes, or lengths of rope
- Traffic cones or trashcans for designating goal areas
- 16 sock balls (or any kind of small, soft balls) per defensive player on each team

▶SETUP

- Distribute sock balls to each player on defense.
- Teams appoint one player each to act as referee.
- Referees have teams play "rock-scissors-paper" to determine which team is offense.
- Teams position themselves at either end of the playing field, in offensive and defensive lines, and in traditional football stances.
- Team in possession kicks off.

▶SAFETY

Alert players that with the sock balls on the ground, there is an increased chance of tripping.

▶COACHING TIPS

- The use of sock balls creates a new strategic element for all players.
- For defense, determining when to throw a sock ball and coordinating with other defensive players become key concerns.
- For offensive players, protecting the player with the football and trying to lure defensive players to waste their sock balls significantly affect the outcome.
- Encourage a "tackled" player to dramatize being tackled.

Toilet-Paper Football

Pairs of toilet paper–tethered players use a toilet-paper roll as a football.

Players run in pairs, connected by toilet paper. Every player must hold onto the end of a length of toilet paper. The team in possession of the toilet-paper roll kicks it downfield, then the other team runs to retrieve it and carry it across the opponent's end zone. The connecting toilet paper cannot touch the ground. Players are "tackled" if their length of toilet paper is torn. If tackled, players may not run, but they can kick the ball when possible. Any player who runs by himself (not connected to another player by a toilet-paper strip) or touches another player trades places with a referee. Players score 6 points by completing a pass in the opponent's end zone (touchdown). The team that scores more points at the end of 20 minutes wins. If there's no score, the team closer to the opponent's end zone wins.

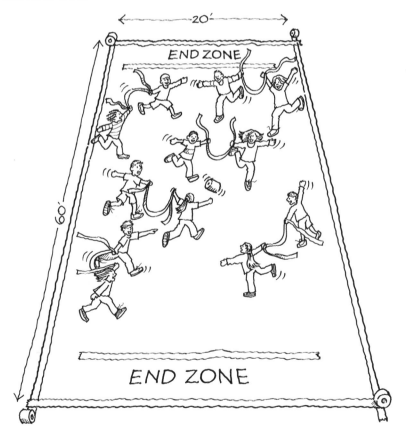

▶*PLAYERS*

Two teams of 4 to 15 players per team.

▶*SPACE*

Football field, soccer field, or any open play space at least 20 feet wide and 60 feet long, with toilet-paper boundaries on all sides.

▶JUNK

· Several rolls of toilet paper

· Whistles or noisemakers for the referees

▶*SETUP*

· The group divides into two teams.

· Each team selects a referee.

· Both teams begin the game at the opposite ends of the field, around the 20-yard line.

· Within each team, pairs of players hold the ends of a 6-foot length of toilet paper.

▶*SAFETY*

Do not allow any movement after the whistle is blown, until the penalty is resolved.

▶*COACHING TIPS*

· A pair of players can easily put themselves out of play if one player lets go of the toilet paper or if they tear it. You might begin this game with some practice running.

· Try playing this with 12-foot or 3-foot lengths of toilet paper.

· If a player disturbs the toilet-paper boundary markers or goal lines, the other team gains posession.

Chess Football

Play football, one move at a time.

At a signal from the referee, teams alternate turns, one player moving at a time. Each player must move as many strides as the number on her headband card. A player that is touched is considered tackled and cannot move until the end of the play. The player with the football can pass instead of moving. If the player with the football is tagged, the ball is "downed" and a new play begins. The goal is to get the football as close as possible to the opposite end zone. The team closer to the end zone at the end of 20 minutes wins.

▶PLAYERS

Two teams of 5 to 11 players per team. This is good for players with mixed or limited movement capabilities.

▶SPACE

An open space about 15 feet wide by 40 feet long. Boundaries are on all sides of the field, marked with anything available (toilet paper, chalk, ribbon) with five-foot-wide goal zones marked in the center of each end.

▶JUNK

- A football or foam football
- Ribbon, index cards, and markers to make headbands

▶SETUP

- Players begin in the center of the field.
- Teams create headbands by writing a number between 3 and 12 on index cards and tying those cards to their heads. Numbers correspond to the mobility of each position that will be played.
- For offense: center, right, left guard; right, left tackle; end, wide receiver; quarterback, halfback, fullback, tailback. For defense: tackles, defensive ends, linebackers, and safeties. These numbers can be assigned

to different positions at the discretion of the team captains. A sample follows:

Offense	Defense
Center: 4	Tackles: 12
Guards: 6	End: 8
Tackles: 6	Linebacker: 8
End: 8	Safety: 6
Wide receiver: 10	
Halfback: 10	
Fullback: 12	
Tailback: 8	

▶ SAFETY

There is no running or tackling in this game, so there are no significant safety considerations.

▶ COACHING TIPS

- Meet collectively to determine the value of each position.
- Encourage players to exercise their understanding of the game and how each position is played.
- After about 10 minutes of play, try having both teams, and all players, make their moves simultaneously. If they do this well and fairly, continue. If not, go back to the one-move-at-a-time rule.
- Allow both teams to huddle between plays to plan their next moves.

Water Football

Keep-away football in the water.

Players can swim or run (as best they can). The player with the ball cannot swim or run; he must pass. The receiver must remain seated. If the receiver misses the ball, the other team gains possession. Both teams resume their positions at opposite ends of the pool. Six points are scored each time the opposing team is able to complete a pass to the receiver. The team with more points at the end of 20 minutes wins. If there's no score, the team closer to the opponent's end zone wins. Players can't touch each other or the ball with their hands, but they may block with their bodies.

▶PLAYERS

Two teams of three to seven players per team. Players with limited mobility can act as receivers.

▶SPACE

Swimming pool.

▶JUNK

- One ball (football, sock ball, sponge ball, Wiffle ball)
- Pool noodles, goggles (both optional)

▶SETUP

- Players begin at either end of the swimming pool. If they are all good swimmers, use the length of the pool. If they're not good swimmers, use the width of the shallow end.
- One player from each team sits on the wall of the pool, behind the opposing team, acting as the receiver.

▶*SAFETY*

The smaller the group, the easier it is to spot people in trouble. Consider starting with a smaller group and then adding a player for each team after each play.

▶*COACHING TIPS*

- You can add both silliness and challenge by having all players sit on pool noodles. Any player who falls off her noodle, so to speak, is considered "tackled."
- If there are goggles for all players, then splashing becomes a much more enjoyable strategy.
- Start out with a football, if you want. But do consider using a sock ball. A wet sock ball has some fascinating properties.

One-Foot Football

Don't run; hop.

Players must hop on one foot while holding the other foot in one hand. Any player with both feet on the ground is out for the remainder of the play. Players may try to knock each other off balance but only with the free hand. Any player who commits a foul changes places with the referee. Players score 6 points by completing a pass in the opponent's end zone (touchdown). The team that scores more points at the end of 20 minutes wins. If there's no score, the team closer to the opponent's end zone wins.

▶PLAYERS

Two teams of 3 to 11 players per team.

▶SPACE

Any open space (football field, beach, playground, gym) no bigger than 15 by 30 feet. Boundaries and goal areas are marked. The goal areas are in the middle of either end zone, approximately the width of the playing area.

▶JUNK

- Beach ball or playground ball at least 18 inches wide
- Boundaries and end zones marked with socks, shoes, toilet paper, lengths of rope
- Traffic cones or trashcans for designating goal areas
- Whistles or noisemakers for each referee

▶SETUP

- The group divides into two teams. Each team selects a referee.
- Both teams begin the game at the opposite ends of the field, around the 20-yard line.

▶ *SAFETY*

Remind players that if they're knocked off balance, it is better to put both feet on the ground and acknowledge that they've been tackled than to allow themselves to fall to the ground.

▶ *COACHING TIPS*

- Referees may need extra support in halting play when a player has both feet on the ground.

- Players who normally use canes, crutches, or wheelchairs do not have to abide by the one-foot rule. Hence, they have an extra strategic value to their team. You might need to point this out.

- If, after 10 minutes or so of play, players are able to maintain balance and safety, consider allowing players to use their whole bodies to unbalance each other.

Base Football

Kickball with tackling.

The offense determines kicking order. The first player stands at home plate, trying to kick the ball as far as possible. Once the ball is kicked, that player attempts to round the bases. The player may stop at any base. As long as the player is standing on a base, he is safe. Any defensive player who has the football may try to tackle the kicker (batter) as long as the kicker is not on base. The tackler merely has to hold onto the player and keep him from moving. A player is considered tackled if he is immobilized for three seconds. Defensive players may pass the ball. The offense tries to score a "home run" by rounding the bases and getting home without getting tackled. If, after the offense kicks the ball, a member of the offense catches it without a bounce, the kicker is out. When the offense gets three outs, teams change positions. Any player committing a foul trades places with a referee. Each home run is 6 points. The team with more points at the end of 20 minutes wins.

▶*PLAYERS*

Two teams of 5 to 11 players per team.

▶*SPACE*

A baseball field, playground, sandlot—wherever a game of baseball can be played.

▶*JUNK*

- Use anything that can be kicked, caught, and passed (a football, kickball, playground ball).
- Make bases out of place mats, pieces of cardboard, or anything flat and not too slippery.

▶*SETUP*

- Players arrange themselves on a baseball diamond. The defense is in the field, and the offense is up to bat.
- Players on each team select one player to be a referee.
- There are defensive players for every base as well as between bases and in the outfield and infield.

▶ *SAFETY*

- Though the game involves tackling, only one player (the ball carrier) can tackle, and only one player (the kicker) can be tackled; therefore, physical risk is minimized. Again, stress that tackling does not mean to throw a player to the ground, but rather to immobilize the player for a count of three.
- Field players need to stay alert to the position of the ball so that they are prepared to receive (and don't get hit by the ball). Players should wear athletic shoes (no cleats).

▶ *COACHING TIPS*

To change the level of challenge, consider increasing or decreasing the size of the diamond or number of bases.

Kick-the-Can Football

Hide-and-seek football.

Players in the offense run and hide. Defensive players try to find them. Any player tagged becomes captured and must stay in the home area. Any free player who is carrying the football may try to throw the football into the cans. If the cans fall, all the players who have been captured are freed, and the offense scores a touchdown. If the player with the football is tagged before she can throw the football, or if she throws and misses, the defense gains possession of the ball. The goal of the offense is to have as many "free" players as possible. The goal of the defense is to capture (tag) the player with the football or as many players in the offensive team as possible. That number (the number of free players) is the team's score. The game is over after 20 minutes of play.

▶PLAYERS

Two teams of three to nine players per team.

▶SPACE

Any fairly open space will work, even if there are trees and other obstacles in the space. A small open space, at least 10 feet in diameter, is needed for the base.

▶JUNK

- Two trashcans, stacked mouth to mouth to form the base
- Two trashcan lids for shields for defensive players
- Socks, toilet paper, ribbon, or something to form the boundaries around the base

▶SETUP

- Set up the trashcans in the middle of a 10-foot-diameter circular base.
- Put boundaries around the trashcans.
- All players start within the boundaries.
- At a signal, all players on the offense run away and hide while the defensive players close their eyes and count. One player on the offense has the ball. Players on that team may secretly pass the ball back and forth to each other while they're in the process of hiding (in case someone

on the defense is peeking) so they can make it harder to spot the ball carrier when the round begins.

▶SAFETY

Caution defensive players to be aware of incoming football throws.

▶COACHING TIPS

- Encourage the offense to coordinate their attack on the base as a team of three or more players, passing the football between them to avoid capture.
- Encourage the defense to cover as much of the field as possible, distributing players so that the home base remains guarded and that team attacks can be covered.
- You might need to define areas that are out of bounds for hiding.
- Playing in a completely open area requires more strategic play from the offense.
- If the offense is playing too defensively (not trying to score), remind them about scoring.

Scooter Football

Keep-away football on wheels.

The ball is punched (as in a volleyball serve) instead of kicked or passed. Players can only roll forward. A team scores 6 points if they can successfully pass the ball to one of their members (the receiver) who is in the opponent's goal zone. The team with the higher score at the end of 20 minutes wins. All players must remain seated on their scooters or skateboards. No physical contact is allowed, except for tagging the player with the ball. Only the player with the ball can be tagged. When the player with the ball is tagged, the next play begins where the player was tagged.

The receiver must stay within the goal zone. No other player may occupy the goal zone. The ball stays in play unless it crosses a boundary. If the player with the ball is able to punch it to the receiver, that team scores. If the receiver misses, the other team gains possession. Players that commit fouls trade places with a referee.

▶PLAYERS

Two teams of 3 to 11 players per team.

▶SPACE

Gym, playground, or any open and paved surface measuring at least 20 by 40 feet.

▶JUNK

- Gym scooters or skateboards for each player
- Boundary and goal markers (e.g., tape, traffic cones)
- Kickball, punch ball, playground ball, or soccer ball

▶SETUP

- Players sit on scooters or skateboards (or a combination of both).
- Teams start at opposite ends of the field.
- Rectangular boundaries are drawn so that there's a space of 3 feet from the walls.
- Traffic cones are set in the center of each end of the field, about 7 feet apart (these are the goal posts).
- Each team selects one member as a referee and another to be the receiver.

▶ *SAFETY*

Caution players to keep their hands off the floor and use feet only to propel themselves.

▶ *COACHING TIPS*

For fun and greater mobility, have two players sit back to back on a scooter or skateboard.

GOAL MARKERS

←—7'—→

40'

20'

Sugar-Pack Football

Catapult the sugar pack into the opponent's end zone.

The offense begins the play by placing the spoon so that the handle is at the edge of the table and the mouth of the spoon is pointing to the opponent; then he places the sugar pack widthwise on the handle of the spoon. The offensive player launches the sugar pack by tapping firmly on the mouth end of the spoon. The offense has four turns. If the offense is successful by the fourth turn and able to launch the sugar pack so that it lands on the opponent's edge of the table with some part of the sugar pack actually over the edge, the offense gets an opportunity to try for a field goal. Off-table-landing sugar packs don't count as a score. If the offense is not successful, the defense gains possession and continues from where the sugar pack last landed. To attempt a field goal, the offense places the spoon in the middle of the table and must launch the sugar pack so that it goes between the salt and pepper shakers. Players score 6 points if any part of the pack is over the edge of the table. Players score an additional point if they score a touchdown and then can launch the pack so that it lands between the salt and pepper shakers.

▶PLAYERS

Two players.

▶SPACE

A dinner table, counter, the floor, any flat surface.

▶JUNK

- A tablespoon and a paper pack of sugar or sugar substitute
- Napkins and salt and pepper shakers to mark boundaries and goals

▶SETUP

- Players sit at opposite ends of the table.
- Use napkins to mark left and right boundaries.
- Use the salt and pepper shakers to mark the goalposts. Set them 6 inches apart, in the center of the table edge, when needed.

▶SAFETY

It can hurt to use your fist on the spoon; that's why players should tap the spoon with a finger. Be sure the table is cleared and ample permissions are granted from the table's owner.

▶COACHING TIPS

- Try different utensils (forks, dessert spoon).
- Try using a slightly wet sugar pack.

CHAPTER 6

Junkyard Basketball

L ike every sport in this collection, basketball has a strong "street" tradition. You find basketball hoops on playgrounds, driveways, backyards, and alleys, as well as on the wall in an office and attached to a trashcan. Basketball could very well be your ideal junkyard-able sport not only because it's ubiquitous but also because it's so easily identified. The following collection of junkyard basketball demonstration games is a good representation of how powerful and adaptable basketball is and how easily we can bring it to new places and players.

Ball-for-All Basketball

A ball for every player.

Each team begins the game in their own basket zone (the semicircular zone by their basket). A team scores 2 points by getting the ball in the opposing team's basket. The team with more points at the end of 20 minutes wins. No physical contact is allowed between players. If a player loses her ball and it crosses the court boundaries, she can't retrieve it. No holding on to the ball—players must either dribble, pass, or shoot their ball at all times, even when standing still. A player can use his free hand to hit a basketball out of another player's hands. It is illegal to throw a ball at another player. If a player gets hit by a ball, she automatically gets a free throw.

▶PLAYERS

Two teams of 3 to 12 players per team.

▶SPACE

Basketball court, gym, or playground.

▶JUNK

- A bouncing ball (basketball, playground ball, beach ball) for every player
- Noisemakers for referees

▶SETUP

- One player from each team is selected as referee.
- Each team begins the game in their own basket zone (the semicircular zone by their basket).
- Every player has a ball.

▶SAFETY

- If playing in a gym, players should have rubber-soled shoes or bare feet.
- Players are liable to get hit by a ball. There is a penalty for this, but players should all be aware of this risk.

▶COACHING TIPS

The first time the game is played, use small beach balls or some other kind of ball that bounces and won't hurt players if it bounces off of them.

Wheelchair Doubles Basketball

Players in pairs riding wheelchariots.

The game begins with two players, one from each team, competing in a tip-off. Other players position themselves so that they are each ready to receive the ball and move it down the court to the opponent's basket. Players score 2 points by getting the ball into the opponent's basket. The team with more points at the end of 20 minutes wins. Wheelers must keep both hands on their chairs at all times. Bouncers must either bounce or throw the ball. No holding the ball. Players who commit fouls exchange places with referees. The fouled player gets a free throw.

▶ *PLAYERS*

Two teams of 2 to 10 players per team.

▶ *SPACE*

- Playground, gym, or any hard-surfaced area at least 12 by 20 feet.
- A basket on either end (anything from a regulation backboard to trash-cans).

▶JUNK

- Wheelchairs, office chairs, even shopping carts (one for every other player)
- A good bouncing ball (at least 6 inches in diameter)
- Cloth (towels, pillowcases, socks) for blindfolds (optional)
- Noisemakers for referees

▶SETUP

- Players work in pairs. One player is the wheeler, the other the bouncer.
- The wheeler can stand behind a chair or sit on the chair. The bouncer can sit on the chair or on the wheeler's lap.
- Each team selects one or two players (one if the sides are uneven) to play referee.

▶SAFETY

Chairs can tip over or collide if there's too much enthusiasm.

▶COACHING TIPS

- Alternate roles where possible (wheelers change position with bouncers).
- Encourage bouncers and wheelers to develop good communication. Wheelers are standing and have a better view of the whole court.
- Try playing it with wheelers or bouncers blindfolded.

Racket Basket

Paddle the ball, hit the backboard.

Two players meet in the center of the court, far enough apart so that they can't hit each other with their rackets. The referee throws the ball straight down so that it bounces up between the two players. Players try to hit the ball toward their teammates (as in a tip-off). A team scores 2 points for hitting the opposing team's backboard, 10 points for hitting the basket. The team with more points at the end of 20 minutes wins. Players cannot touch the ball or each other. A player cannot hit another player with a racket. When a referee spots a foul, all play must stop. Players must keep the ball bouncing (no carrying the ball on the racket), but the ball doesn't have to bounce on the floor. A fouled player has the option of a free throw or of asking the player who fouled to exchange positions with a referee.

▶PLAYERS

Two teams of three to five players per team.

▶SPACE

Basketball court (indoors or outdoors).

▶JUNK

- A racket of any kind (e.g., tennis racket or Ping-Pong paddle) for each person
- Some kind of ball that bounces well (Super Ball, Ping-Pong ball, jacks ball, silicone juggling balls, beach ball)

▶SETUP

- Each team appoints a referee.
- Each player has a racket.
- Teams stand on either side of the two starting players, up- and down-court.

▶SAFETY

- Be careful that players don't hit each other with rackets. Be quick to respond.
- If playing in a gym, players should wear either rubber-soled shoes or play in bare feet.

▶COACHING TIPS

- Start with a larger ball that is easier to see, such as a beach ball.
- Start with a shorter-handled paddle, perhaps a Ping-Pong paddle.
- Try it with two paddles for each player.
- If there's any problem with players hitting each other with rackets, make it a rule that players can't run, but take only one step (keeping one foot in place).

Trash Basketball

Basketball with a paper wad and two moveable trashcans for baskets.

The team in possession of the ball gets 2 points every time they successfully get the ball in its basket. The team with the higher score at the end of 20 minutes wins. The trashcan carriers must stay within their zones. They can run with their trashcan and raise or lower it as they desire. If playing with a ball that doesn't bounce, players may not run with the ball. If the ball does bounce, players must dribble the ball while moving. Players cannot cross into the basket zone. Players cannot touch each other.

▶PLAYERS

Two teams of 3 to 10 players per team.

▶SPACE

Trash Basketball can be played on almost any open playing area, from 8 by 12 feet to regulation dimensions—basketball court, gym, playground, any open area. If players use a bouncing ball, the area should have a hard surface.

The field is divided into two or three zones (depending on whether you're playing on a half or full court). For a simple game on a half court, one zone is for the playing area, and the other is for the basket (trashcan) carriers. For a larger game on a full court, one zone is the playing area and one zone on each end is a basket zone (for a total of three zones). The boundaries for the basket area should be no more than a quarter of the court. The basket carrier can only travel within the basket zone (so that there's always a separation between the players and the basket carriers).

▶JUNK

- One or more trashcans or shopping carts for baskets.
- The ball can be anything—wads of paper, sock balls, basketballs, playground balls.
- Chalk, traffic cones, toilet paper—anything to safely mark the boundaries and basket zones.

▶SETUP

A trash basket and trash basket carrier are positioned in the basket zones at either end of the playing area (if playing full court).

▶SAFETY

Players should wear rubber-soled shoes or be barefoot if on a hard surface.

▶COACHING TIPS

- Be sure the separation between the basket carrier and the players is wide enough to keep it a meaningful contest.
- Players should not be able to simply reach into the basket without throwing.
- If the basket carrier is in a wheelchair, he may opt to have a pusher.
- Remind players that there is no touching at all—no part of any player's body may touch anyone else.
- If people have trouble following the rules, have each team assign a player to be a referee. Then the rule is that if someone fouls, that player changes positions with a referee, or the player who was fouled gets a free throw.

All-Terrain Basketball

Play anywhere, but don't run.

Each team has one ball, and only the players who have the ball can move their feet. Players score 2 points every time they get the ball through the opponent's goal. The team with the higher score at the end of 20 minutes wins. Players with possession of the ball can take up to three steps and have the option of shooting or passing.

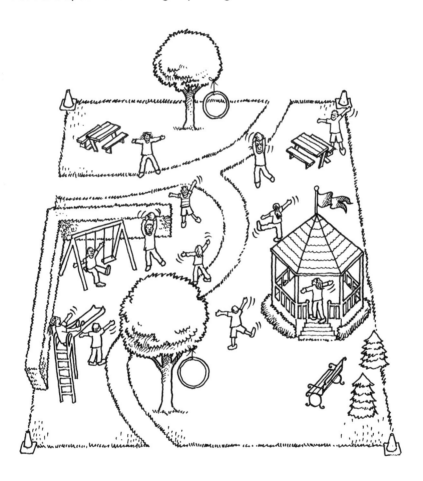

Musical Basketless Basketball

Group juggling.

The goal of this game is to build a complex motion without losing a ball. The more complex the motion, the better. One player starts. That player bounces the ball in some manner (change hands, turn around, toss and catch, bounce twice, and so on). All players perform the motion in the same way, simultaneously, and continue performing that motion until someone misses the ball or everyone agrees that the game is over. The next player adds a motion, performing both motions either in sequence or simultaneously. All players then imitate that player, until everyone has had a turn, or a ball is missed, or everyone wants to stop.

▶*PLAYERS*

At least 5 players and as many as 50 players.

▶*SPACE*

Any open area with a hard surface at least 10 feet in diameter.

▶*JUNK*

- A basketball for each player
- A boom box with appropriately funky music

▶*SETUP*

- Break the group into groups of 10 or fewer.
- Players stand in a circle, and each player has a basketball.

▶*SAFETY*

Once players add a passing motion to the mix, things can get a little threatening (balls flying everywhere simultaneously).

▶*COACHING TIPS*

- Encourage players to use the music; it makes it easier to keep a rhythm and makes the game more fun.
- Have groups demonstrate their completed "dance" to one another.

Air Basketball

Basketball with a balloon.

Cardboard cartons serve as goals for this game. Players score 2 points by getting the balloon to stay in the top carton. The team with the higher score at the end of 20 minutes, or when the game ends, wins. The balloon cannot touch the ground. If the balloon goes out of bounds or pops, the team of the player who last touched the balloon loses possession. The other team throws it back in to one of their players. Players cannot touch other players. Since there are no referees, players should call their own fouls. The game ends if a carton stack is knocked over.

▶ *PLAYERS*

Two teams of three to five players per team.

▶ *SPACE*

Any flat, open space at least 15 by 40 feet.

▶ *JUNK*

- Balloons or beach balls
- Materials for marking boundaries (e.g., chalk, tape, traffic cones)
- Cardboard cartons for making goals (enough to stack at least seven feet high), and the top carton is open on the top and wide enough for the balloon to enter

▶ *SETUP*

- Stack the cartons on either end of the playing field so that they are approximately where the baskets would be.
- Players gather in the middle of the field.
- One player from each team gets in position for the tip-off.

▶ *SAFETY*

- If playing outside, take the wind into account; try using a beach ball instead of a balloon.
- Players tend to look up often, and they might inadvertently run into each other. If the player with the ball is hit, it should count as a foul, and that player should be given a free throw.

▶*COACHING TIPS*

- The stability of the carton stacks can become an issue, especially if there is a wind. If it becomes a problem, consider rescinding the rule about the game ending if a carton stack is knocked over. Stop the game and have the players restack the cartons, but let them know that the clock is still running.

- If players are successful at self-policing, you can eliminate the need for referees altogether. This is beneficial to the spirit of the game, so do what you can to recognize openness and honesty.

- Using a beach ball makes the game less funny but more competitive.

Paper-Wad Basketball

Toss paper wads into cups.

The goal of this game is to toss a wad into an opponent's cup or glass. The first player to achieve the goal wins the round. Play as many rounds as everyone wants. The player with the highest total wins then wins the game. Players toss wads simultaneously and can score only by getting their paper wads into the cup or glass of the player sitting on the opposite side.

Players can attempt to deflect each other's paper wads by hitting a wad in flight with another wad. Paper wads that fall off the table are out of play. If someone touches a wad in flight with her hand, it is a foul. A fouled player gets a free throw (no one else is throwing during the foul shot).

▶ PLAYERS

Two to six players.

▶ SPACE

Tabletop (at a restaurant, at home, in the cafeteria, on the floor).

▶ JUNK

- Glasses or cups
- Wadded paper napkins, tissues, or sheets of paper

▶ SETUP

- Players sit opposite each other. If there are four players, each would sit at his or her own side of a square table.
- In front of each player is an empty glass.
- Each player makes an agreed-on number of paper wads (two to six).

▶SAFETY

Make sure there's nothing breakable on the table, and make sure there's no one nearby who would be too disturbed by this frolic.

▶COACHING TIPS

- The tighter the wad, the better.
- Consider the virtues of wad wetting.
- This game can be played anywhere, outdoors or indoors. It can be played with balls and boxes, beanbags and hula hoops, pebbles and holes in the ground.
- Players can increase or decrease the distance between them when setting up.
- Try it with more or fewer players, younger and older.

Basebasket

Dribbling trashcan baseball.

The field is a baseball diamond made of trashcans, with teams in the out-field and at bat. The goal is to score a home run by touching every base in order and then returning home. The team with more home runs at the end of 20 minutes wins. The batter hits the ball as in a volleyball serve. If the ball is caught before it hits the ground, the batter is out and the other team is up to bat. The team in the field must dribble or pass the ball (no running with the ball unless while dribbling). To get a player out, the ball must be inside the trashcan of the base she's running toward. A runner may not run back to a previous base. If a runner makes it to a base before the ball, that runner is safe, and the next player on her team is up. There is no physical contact between players.

▶ PLAYERS

Two teams of 3 to 11 players per team.

▶ SPACE

Gym or playground or any open, ball-bounceable surface big enough for a small baseball diamond. The space should be 30 by 30 feet or more.

▶ JUNK

- Four trashcans or open cartons big enough to contain the ball
- A playground ball or beach ball

▶ SETUP

- Make a baseball diamond of sorts—put a trashcan at home plate, first, second, and third base. No pitcher's mound is needed.
- One team is in the outfield, positioned at and between bases; the other team is up to bat.

▶*SAFETY*

If players are outdoors, running on a hard surface is always hazardous. Players should be dressed appropriately (long pants and long-sleeved shirts, soft-soled shoes).

▶*COACHING TIPS*

- If you use a beach ball, you can make the field smaller (20 by 20 feet).
- If it's too hard for players to get the ball into the trashcan, make it a rule that they can just knock the trashcan over.

Wall Basketball

Bounce the ball against the wall first.

Players take turns trying to bounce the ball against the wall so that it goes into the basket. A successful throw scores 2 points. The player with the highest score at the end of 20 minutes wins. Players take turns throwing from the throwing line. The ball must hit the wall and then go into the basket. If the ball hits the basket first, or if the basket is knocked over, that player's turn is over. If the player succeeds, she gets another throw.

▶PLAYERS

Two or more players.

▶SPACE

A hard-surfaced area (gym floor or paved area) at least 10 feet wide by 20 feet long, adjoining a blank wall at least 10 feet wide and 10 feet high.

▶JUNK

- Two trashcans or cardboard cartons large enough to hold a minibasketball
- Six minibasketballs or inflatable balls about 4 to 6 inches in diameter
- Tape or chalk to mark the throwing line

▶SETUP

- Build the basket by stacking two trashcans together, the bottom trashcan mouth down and the top one mouth up (or do the same with cardboard cartons).
- Position the target about 3 feet away from the wall.
- Draw a throwing line about 10 feet away from the wall.

▶SAFETY

Be sure the area is well cleared behind the players in case the ball bounces beyond their catch and they run to retrieve it.

▶COACHING TIPS

Encourage players to explore variations: Move the "basket" farther away or closer to the wall, move the throwing line farther away, build a higher basket, throw underhanded, throw backward, and so on.

Ring Around the Basketball

Teams compete to develop a ball-bouncing routine.

The goal of this game is to create a "routine" that is too difficult for others to perform. Each team creates a routine. The other teams then take turns trying to replicate that routine. The team that creates a routine that the fewest number of other teams can perform then wins. Team members must be continuously in motion—no standing still. The ball must bounce at least once inside the hula hoop before another player catches it. A different player must return the ball each time.

▶*PLAYERS*

Two to six groups, two to six players per group.

▶*SPACE*

Any hard surface (gym floor or playground). You'll need a circle, at least 8 feet in diameter, per team.

▶*JUNK*

- A hula hoop for each team
- Two basketballs for each team

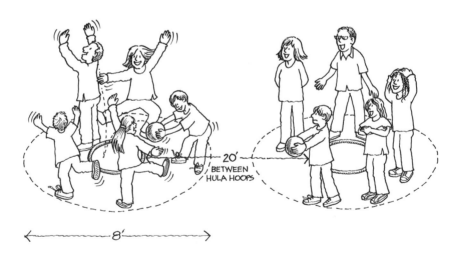

20'
BETWEEN
HULA HOOPS

8'

▶SETUP

- Place hula hoops on the ground about 20 feet apart (far enough from each other so that each team can develop its routine).
- Each team is given two basketballs and assigned a hula hoop.
- Each team stands equidistant around their hula hoop.

▶SAFETY

Teams should be alert for stray balls.

▶COACHING TIPS

- Encourage players to master each step before adding a new step.
- If they get stuck, help them try different strategies: changing directions, changing hands, turning around, clapping hands, clapping each other's hands together.

Scoot Basketball

Sit-and-slide basketball.

Players move by scooting backward. Players score 2 points for getting the ball in the opposing team's basket. The team with more points at the end of 20 minutes wins. Players must remain seated on their towels at all times.

▶ PLAYERS

Two teams of two or more players per team.

▶ SPACE

Any smooth polished surface (gym, hallway, cafeteria) with an open space at least 20 by 20 feet.

▶ JUNK

- Bath towels for each player
- Established basketball baskets or baskets made out of trashcans or cardboard cartons
- Basketball, playground ball, or small beach ball

▶ SETUP

- If there are no baskets available, create one on each end of the court, or just play on half court.
- Each player sits on a towel and is barefoot.
- One player from each team meets in the center for the tip-off.

▶ SAFETY

Scooting backward is a collision-prone activity. Luckily, you can't scoot very fast. But some words to the wise could help players avoid headaches.

▶ COACHING TIPS

- Rubber-soled shoes or bare feet definitely give players an advantage.
- Make sure players stay on their towels. If this game works well for them, think about using gym scooters instead.
- Players should be dribbling or passing at all times. Maintaining a good dribble is definitely a challenge when they're that low to the ground.

CHAPTER 7

Junkyard Baseball

There may be more junkyard-like versions of baseball than of any other sport. From the early part of the 20th century, children played games such as half-ball, stickball, wall ball, and stoopball. City kids, especially in Philadelphia and New York, played most of these games. Half-ball was played, as the name implies, with half a ball and a stick at a time when there was a certain kind of ball (a "pinkie" or "spaldeen") that tended to break in half. A Web site is devoted to this game: www.halfball.com. Then there's stickball (www.streetplay.com/stickball/), which was played when kids couldn't find or afford a bat. In fact, there's a Major Stickball League; go to www.stick-ball.com. And before that, there was stoolball, an English game in which milkmaids would place two stools on their sides at either end of the playing field. Pitchers would throw a ball at the stool, while batters tried to hit the ball and keep it from hitting the stool (this game became rounders and then cricket). Then there's tipcat, a game that was purportedly played in early Egypt. Instead of a ball, kids used a stick, called the "cat," that was pointed at both ends. The cat was put on the ground and struck sharply on one of the ends with a stick. This would launch it in the air so that the player could then hit it with the stick like a baseball. The downside of this game is that the other players were supposed to try to catch it.

Dodgeball Baseball

Throw the ball at the runner to get her out.

This game is the same as baseball, except that players can try to hit a runner (as long as she's not on base) with the ball; this is the only way to get a runner out. Start with bases loaded (one runner on each base). Players score runs by running the bases without getting tagged or hit by the ball. The team with the higher score after 20 minutes (10-minute time limit per inning) of play wins. A runner who is hit is out. Three strikes retires the hitter, and three outs retires the side.

▶*PLAYERS*

Two teams of three to nine players per team.

▶*SPACE*

Any open field, preferably dirt or grass, at least 20 by 30 feet.

▶*JUNK*

- A five-sock sock ball, Wiffle ball, or mini-soccer ball—any baseball-sized ball that's soft enough so that it won't hurt when a player gets hit by it. It's a good idea to have a bunch of balls ready, just in case.
- Boundary markers are traffic cones, toilet paper, chalk, rope, yard, ribbon, climbing webbing, or socks.
- Base markers are sandbags, place mats, towels, or traffic cones.
- A broomstick, Wiffle bat, or any kind of bat can be used.

▶*SETUP*

- Create a baseball diamond with bases about 15 feet apart.
- The outfield surrounds the diamond, extending the playing area an additional 10 feet.
- The pitcher and catcher as well as all field positions can be used.
- Start with bases loaded—one runner on each base.

▶*SAFETY*

Caution players about handing the bat off to the next player rather than throwing it.

▶*COACHING TIPS*

If it's too easy to get someone out, decrease the distance between bases.

Prisoner's Baseball

Players who are tagged out are in "prison" at the base where they were tagged.

When the batter hits the ball, if it gets caught before it hits the ground, the player is out. If the ball doesn't get caught, the batter tries to reach the closest base without getting tagged by a player with the ball. If a runner is tagged, he stays at the base where he was tagged, and he is in "prison." If a runner makes it to a base without getting tagged and other players from his side are already in prison, those players are free to try to get to the next base. If a freed player gets to a base where players are in prison, all are freed to try to make it to the next base. If a freed player gets tagged before he gets "home," he is in prison at home. If a freed player makes it home without getting tagged, he and all the players at home plate score a run. If everyone is in prison, that side retires.

The goal is to try to free players who have been caught, get as many home runs as possible by hitting the ball within the foul lines in such a way that no one can catch it, and get to a base without getting tagged by a player with the ball. The team with the higher score at the end of 20 minutes (10-minute time limit per inning) wins. When a ball is missed, the batter gets a strike against him. Three strikes, and he's out.

▶PLAYERS

Two teams of 3 to 20 players per team.

▶SPACE

Any open field, preferably dirt or grass, at least 20 by 30 feet.

▶JUNK

- For a ball, use a five-sock sock ball, Wiffle ball, or mini-soccer ball— something soft enough to catch without gloves.
- Boundary markers are traffic cones, toilet paper, chalk, rope, yard, ribbon, climbing webbing, or socks.
- Base markers are sandbags, place mats, towels, or traffic cones.
- A broomstick, Wiffle bat, or any kind of bat can be used.

▶SETUP

- Set up at least two bases, and as many as five, along the traditional diamond.

- Players in the field assume traditional positions: a player at each base, shortstops between, outfielders behind, a pitcher, and catcher.
- The batter is at home plate.

▶SAFETY

A lot of players can be running in the field. The more players there are, the more danger there is that someone will run into someone else.

▶COACHING TIPS

- If the group is too large, add more bases.
- The more prisoners there are, the more fun it is when they all get released.
- The mayhem factor might at first appear daunting, but it's really a big payoff for everyone.

Get the ball and tag anyone who is not in her base.

All players stand inside their bases (hoops), except for the batter, who has no hoop. The batter bats the ball. As soon as the ball hits the ground, all players race to retrieve the ball while the batter runs to any unoccupied hoop. Once someone has the ball, any player not standing in a base can get tagged by the player with the ball. If someone gets tagged, the player who tagged her becomes the next batter. Only one player can stand in a base.

The goal of the game is to be the batter. There is no score and really no winner.

▶PLAYERS

Five or more players.

▶SPACE

An open field or gym. The size of the space depends on the number of players. For 10 players, you'd want a space about 30 feet in diameter.

▶JUNK

- Use a Wiffle ball or foam ball.
- Bases are hula hoops (one fewer than the number of players).
- The bat is a Wiffle bat or plastic bat.

▶SETUP

- Place the bases (hoops) in a circle 10 or more feet apart from each other. Leave an opening for the batter.
- Every player stands in a base.
- The batter stands in the opening.

▶SAFETY

Be sure people are wearing nonslip shoes. Don't let people run until the ball has landed, or you can get people running into each other or getting hit by the ball.

▶COACHING TIPS

- Vary the distance between bases to increase or decrease the challenge.
- Encourage players to make a real effort to get the ball (no "base sticking").

Schmerltz Baseball

Players throw a Schmerltz using no bats, no gloves, and more bases.

The player up to bat throws the Schmerltz as far as possible, trying to get it to land somewhere within bounds where there are no players. As soon as the Schmerltz is thrown, that player runs for first base. Players in the field attempt to catch the Schmerltz. The player who is holding the Schmerltz can either tag the runner or tag the base the runner is trying to reach; in either case, the runner is out. If a player catches the Schmerltz before it hits the ground, the thrower is out. A player scores a home run by rounding the bases before he gets tagged. The team with the higher score at the end of 20 minutes (10-minute time limit per inning) wins. Two outs retire the side.

▶PLAYERS

Two teams of three to nine players per team.

▶SPACE

Any open field at least 20 by 30 feet. A dirt or grassy field is safer than asphalt or concrete.

▶JUNK

- A Schmerltz (knee sock with tennis ball, 3- to 6-inch rubber ball, or beanbag in the toe)
- Six bases (sandbags, place mats, traffic cones, carpet squares, towels)
- Boundary markers (traffic cones, toilet paper, chalk, rope, yard, ribbon, climbing webbing, socks)

▶SETUP

- Place three to five bases anywhere in the playing field, and one base for home plate.
- Place boundary markers around the playing area.
- One player from the team that is up to bat stands on the home plate with the Schmerltz in his hand.

- There are no pitchers or catchers.
- The team in the field positions itself near and between the bases and in the outfield.

▶SAFETY

As long as there is running, there is a need for players to exercise some caution. Since the Schmerltz tends to go rather high, players might be too focused on getting the ball to notice that they're in danger of running into someone or something.

▶COACHING TIPS

- The more bases there are, the more players you need to watch, the easier it is to tag someone out, and the higher the score potential.
- Since it's more difficult to catch the Schmerltz by the end, you can make it a rule that if a Schmerltz is caught by the tail before it hits the ground, the side retires.
- Let the players determine how many bases to have and where they want to position them. Consider making that choice the prerogative of the team that's up to bat.

Frisbee Baseball

Tossing a Frisbee instead of batting a ball.

The batter tries to score a run by throwing the Frisbee so that it doesn't get caught, and touching every base in succession without getting tagged. ("Skipping" the Frisbee so that it hits the ground first is legal.) As soon as an outfielder catches the Frisbee, the player with the Frisbee either runs to tag the runner or throws the Frisbee to someone else in the field. Once the Frisbee is caught, only the player with the Frisbee can run. If the batter throws the Frisbee so that it crosses a foul line, that batter is out. If the batter is tagged before reaching a base, the batter is out. Two outs retires the side. The team with the higher score at the end of 20 minutes (10-minute time limit per inning) wins.

▶PLAYERS

Two teams of three to nine players per team.

▶SPACE

- Baseball diamond or open field, at least 15 by 30 feet
- Four bases
- Foul lines marked on either side of the diamond

▶JUNK

- Frisbee
- Toilet paper
- Paper plates, carpet squares, towels, or something else to mark bases

▶SETUP

- There's no pitcher or catcher.
- All other players are in traditional positions—next to each base, short-stop, and outfield.

- Mark foul lines with toilet paper.
- Use paper plates, carpet squares, towels, or something else to mark bases.

▶ SAFETY

On a windy day, the Frisbee may be difficult to control. Be careful of observers and passers-by. If people get hit with the Frisbee, consider using a softer Frisbee.

▶ COACHING TIPS

- Controlling a Frisbee is not the same as throwing a ball. Give the team in the field an opportunity to warm up by passing the Frisbee from base to base.
- If the batters are tagged out too easily, make it a rule that there's no running with the Frisbee.

Cricket Bowling Baseball

Pitcher bowls, batter defends.

The pitcher (bowler) rolls the ball toward the bowling pins. The batter attempts to hit the ball before it reaches the bowling pins. If the batter fails, the field team scores 1 point for each pin knocked down, and then becomes the batting team. If the batter succeeds, she takes the bat with her. Then she must try to run and touch either first or third base with the bat and return to the home plate without getting tagged. If she succeeds, her team scores 1 point for each pin standing, and a new player on that team goes up to bat. The team with the higher score at the end of 20 minutes (10-minute time limit per inning) wins. Teams change positions after two outs.

▶*PLAYERS*

Two teams of three to nine players per team.

▶*SPACE*

A flat, open space at least 30 feet wide by 20 feet long.

▶*JUNK*

- Boundary markers are traffic cones, toilet paper, chalk, rope, yardsticks, ribbon, climbing webbing, or socks.
- Base markers are sandbags, place mats, traffic cones, or towels.
- The ball can be a mini-soccer ball, mini-playground ball, tennis ball, or socks.
- Bowling pins are plastic soda bottles or milk bottles (placed mouth-side down), toilet-paper tubes, or paper-towel tubes.
- The bat can be a cricket bat or tennis racket.

▶*SETUP*

- Set up the bowling pins where home plate would be.
- The batter stands in front of the pins, no farther than 5 feet away.
- Set up bases in the first- and third-base positions.

- The pitcher stands on the pitcher's mound (or closer, depending on abilities).
- Players in the field stand in the normal baseball positions—one at each base, shortstops between, infield and outfield.

▶SAFETY

There is no physical contact in this game. If a softball is used, consider giving baseball gloves to the players in the field.

▶COACHING TIPS

- Encourage the batters to use the first- and third-base choice strategically and to be careful handing the bat to the next player so that the player gets it in time.
- Consider making it a rule that the ball can only be rolled, never thrown—especially if players raise safety concerns.
- If the team in the field scores too easily, move the pitcher's mound farther back.

Playground Baseball

Bounce the ball so hard and high that no one can catch it.

The batter throws the ball down on the ground so that it bounces into the field. The other players try to catch the ball before it hits the ground again. The player who is successful in catching the ball becomes the next batter. Every time the players in the field fail to catch the ball by its second bounce, the batter scores a point (a run) and gets to bat again. The batter's goal is to bounce the ball so hard, high, and far that no one can catch it. The player with the most points at the end of 20 minutes (10-minute time limit per inning) wins.

▶ *PLAYERS*

Two or more players.

▶ *SPACE*

Any open space with a hard surface at least 10 by 20 feet.

▶ *JUNK*

Use a playground ball, maybe a mini-soccer ball, a "pinkie," or a Super Ball.

▶ *SETUP*

- The batter stands at one end of the playing area. The rest of the players stand anywhere from 10 to 20 feet away.
- No boundaries or bases need to be established.

▶ *SAFETY*

Since this is played in the open, on a playground with no boundary markers, players need to pay special attention to bystanders and passers-by so that no one runs into anyone else.

▶ *COACHING TIPS*

- If the batter is scoring too many runs, consider the following variation: If the ball bounces once before being caught, the batter scores a run; if it bounces twice, the batter scores a two-base hit and an imaginary player is on second; if it bounces three times, the batter scores a single.
- If the batter is scoring too few runs, consider changing the ball to something more challenging to catch—a smaller rubber ball, perhaps even a Super Ball.

Baseball on a tennis court.

The batter uses a tennis racket to hit the ball over the net as far as possible within the boundaries of the field, and then runs the bases counterclockwise. The ball must pass over the net to be considered good, otherwise it's a foul. The team in the field attempts to return the ball to the player closest to the runner, who either tags the runner with the ball or tags the base the runner is trying to reach. Players in the field cannot move their feet. The runner holds onto the racket, even while running, and may use the racket to attempt to deflect the ball away from herself or another player. As in baseball, the goal is to hit a home run or to reach the home plate. An interim goal is to reach each of the bases. The team that is up to bat scores 1 point for each completed run. The team that has more points at the end of 20 minutes (10-minute time limit per inning) wins.

▶*PLAYERS*

Two teams of three to nine players per team.

▶*SPACE*

Tennis court, playground, open field (with a surface hard enough for a tennis ball to bounce on). The official dimensions of a tennis court, for doubles play, are 36 by 78 feet; however, the court could be as small as 20 by 40 feet.

▶*JUNK*

- A tennis racket
- A used (somewhat "dead") tennis ball or other similarly sized bouncing ball
- Two sandbags or towels for home plate and second base
- Boundary marking stuff if needed (rope, toilet paper, chalk, string, traffic cones)
- A tennis net, toilet paper, rubber bands, or rope tied between two stands

BOUNDARY BEYOND TENNIS COURT

▶SETUP

- Place a base in the middle of either baseline. One is for home plate, the other for second base.
- First base is the pole holding up the tennis net, to the batter's right. Second base is on the other side of the net, in the center of the opposing team's foul line. Third is the pole to the batter's left.
- One player from the team that is up to bat stands with one foot on the home base.

- The players from the other team are positioned at each remaining base and as shortstops and fielders as in baseball. Outfield is beyond the baseline.
- Boundaries are beyond the tennis court, up to an additional 20 feet beyond and 10 feet to either side.
- Boundaries should be marked.
- There is no catcher or pitcher.

▶SAFETY

Be sure that players who are guarding the bases are at least 2 feet away from the bases so that no one runs into them.

▶COACHING TIPS

- To make the game faster, use more balls. The rule is that as soon as one player hits the ball, that player leaves the racket for the next player and starts running. The next player takes the racket, positions herself at the home plate, and then hits—while the first player is still running.
- Try different variations of how the ball can be hit: under the net, bounced over the net, underhanded.

Waterball

Wet and wacky baseball—and maybe muddy, too.

As in baseball, the players up to bat attempt to hit the ball so that it can't be returned, and then they run the bases while the players in the field attempt to catch the ball or tag the runner before he gets to base. When rounding the bases, the runner must jump into each wading pool. When running between third and home, the runner must slide. After hitting the ball, the runner picks up a water balloon from a teammate. The runner may use the water balloon at any time to get others wet.

The team with more runs at the end of 20 minutes (10-minute time limit per inning) wins.

▶PLAYERS

Two teams of three to nine players per team.

▶SPACE

Dirt or grass field at least 20 by 30 feet.

▶JUNK

- Three small wading pools (one for each base except home)
- A Slip 'N Slide (or long wet plastic sheet) between third and home
- Wiffle bat or plastic bat
- Wiffle ball or sponge ball
- Hose attached to a water source
- Water balloons (6-inch balloons filled with water)
- Towels

▶SETUP

- Place a small wading pool at each base.
- Set up a Slip 'N Slide between third base and home.
- Station players as pitcher, catcher, basemen, shortstop, and fielders. One player from the other team is up to bat.
- Prepare a collection of water balloons.

▶SAFETY

Players should run in bare feet. The field should be cleared of anything that would hurt bare feet. The areas around the bases tend to get muddy and slippery.

▶COACHING TIPS

- The fun of the game has a lot to do with how muddy you get. That's why you'll need a hose with running water and some towels so that players can get unmuddied enough to play more.
- The water balloon idea is to give the runner an added defensive measure and let the people in the field get a taste of all that wetness. If it works, consider giving the pitcher a water balloon as well.

Golf Baseball

Bases are like holes in golf, and bats are like golf clubs.

The first player stands in the middle of the home hula hoop and "tees off" by hitting the ball toward the first-base hoop. The next player follows, and the next after. The first player then picks up the ball from where it landed, placing one foot on the exact spot where the ball had rested, and then hits the ball again toward the first-base hoop.

The game continues in this manner, each player hitting the ball once until all players have reached the home hoop. Each player should hit the ball so that it lands in each hula hoop in succession.

The winner is the player who rounds the bases—getting the ball in each of the hula hoops in order—in the fewest number of hits.

▶PLAYERS

One or more players.

▶SPACE

An open field. No boundary markers or bases needed. Use as much space as is available.

▶JUNK

- Four hula hoops
- Wiffle balls (one for each player)
- Wiffle bats (one for each player)

▶SETUP

Place hula hoops on the ground, like a baseball base, in a diamond configuration—the more space, the bigger the diamond.

▶SAFETY

- Be sure players are positioned so that they're least likely to get hit by someone else's ball.
- If there are too many players, consider adding another diamond in the opposite direction so that there are two intersecting diamonds meeting at home hoop.

▶COACHING TIPS

- The distance between hoops affects the difficulty of the challenge. Increase or decrease accordingly.
- The same game can be played with different equipment—tennis rackets and tennis balls, Schmerltzes, broomsticks, and sock balls.

Hallball

Hit the base to score.

Three trashcans are placed as bases, on their sides with the openings facing the batter. The ball is placed on the floor. The batter uses the Schmerltz to hit the ball toward any one of the target cans. (The goal is to hit the undefended can.) If a player hits the cans he gets a base hit (one, two, or three bases depending on what base is hit); if he gets the ball in the can he gets a home run. If a player can catch the ball before it hits or enters the can, the player switches roles with the batter. If the batter misses the can, the batter is out, and all the players rotate counterclockwise. Players in the field can move only one of their feet. The player with the most home runs at the end of 20 minutes (10-minute time limit per inning) wins.

▶*PLAYERS*

Two to seven players.

▶*SPACE*

A hallway or any relatively narrow space (at least 6 feet wide and 20 feet long) with walls on either side.

▶*JUNK*

- The bat is a Schmerltz (a knee sock with a tennis ball in the toe).
- The ball is a sock ball, Wiffle ball, or mini-soccer ball.
- The bases are trashcans or cardboard boxes.

▶*SETUP*

- Place trashcans about 15 feet away from the batter, one on either side of the hallway (first and third bases) and one in the middle, about 20 feet away. The trashcans are on their sides with the openings facing the batter.
- One player is at each trashcan.
- Two players are in the field.

▶SAFETY

Watch out for passers-through. Since the batter is out if someone catches the ball before it hits the can, even if the ball never leaves the ground or hits the ground first, batters should be encouraged to keep the ball low.

▶COACHING TIPS

- Increase or decrease distances to the bases to increase or decrease the challenge.
- The people at the bases should straddle the cans or boxes to keep them from moving.

Box Baseball

A traditional junkyard game—bounce the ball into the opponent's square to pitch. The opponent uses his hand to hit.

The pitcher throws underhand so that the ball bounces in the square immediately in front of the batter. The batter hits the ball with his hand so that the ball bounces in the square immediately in front of the pitcher. If the ball bounces in the pitcher's box, it's a hit. If the pitcher catches it before it bounces, or if it lands outside the pitcher's box, it's an out.

After three outs the players switch roles. The pitcher tries to pitch the ball so that the batter cannot return it successfully. The player with more hits wins.

▶PLAYERS

In pairs, 2 to 20. Many games can be played simultaneously.

▶SPACE

A sidewalk or a playground.

▶JUNK

- A good bouncing ball that's easy to catch: a mini-soccer ball or mini-basketball, a "pinkie" or a "spaldeen," but probably not a Super Ball.
- Sidewalk chalk (if playing on concrete)

▶SETUP

- The field is three sidewalk squares long.
- Players stand outside the field, at either end, facing each other.
- If players won't be playing on a sidewalk, draw the squares with chalk.

▶SAFETY

Be sure that the area behind each player is clear.

▶COACHING TIPS

- The game is the most fun when players don't pause between throws. Encourage the pitcher to throw again as soon as the ball is returned.
- The middle square is not used. To make the game easier for the pitcher, make it a rule that the batter must get the ball to bounce in the middle square as well as in the pitcher's square.
- Consider lengthening the field by two squares and trying it with a Super Ball (very challenging).

CHAPTER 8

Junkyard Hockey

Hockey is another one of those games that people get dressed up for in protective clothing like helmets and face masks, knee and elbow pads. This can add to the fun as well as the fantasy, so consider adding suitable costume-making junk to your junk repertoire.

Traditionally, there's a lot of body contact in the game of hockey. In junkyard hockey, however, all the ideas described involve little or no physical contact, because the key to a successful experience of junkyard sports is that the experience stays well within the boundaries of fun, and people who get hurt tend to lose their sense of humor very rapidly.

In the hockey demonstration game collection there is one game that is, in fact, quite dangerous. It's called Skateboard Hockey, and it appears on page 145. I had to include it, despite its dangers, because it could really be fun, with the proper cautions, and it can be made a lot safer, if necessary.

Broom Hockey

Hockey played with brooms and a ball.

The game starts with a face-off. Every time a team scores, the game is started again with another face-off. A goal is scored by hitting the ball through the opponent's, um, goal. Only the broom can be used to hit the ball. The ball has to go between and past the goalposts to score. The team with the most goals at the end of 20 minutes wins. No physical contact is allowed between players.

▶PLAYERS

Two teams of three to six players per team.

▶SPACE

The official size of the rink is 200 feet long and 85 feet wide. The corners are rounded in the arc of a circle with a radius of 28 feet. But broom hockey is not that official, and it can be played on the street (streets are usually about 30 feet wide) or playground, lawn, vacant lot, or even in an ice rink. How about 20 feet wide by, say, 50 feet long? There's a goal at either end, usually about 6 feet wide. There's a line down the middle of the field.

▶JUNK

- Line markers are chalk, tape, or maybe just some traffic cones.
- Goal markers are plastic milk bottles, traffic cones (of a different color if you're using traffic cones to mark the boundaries and centerline), trashcans, or cardboard cartons.
- Sticks are brooms. Any kind of broom will work, though the shorter the broom part, the better. Push brooms work, too.
- The ball can be a tennis ball, sock ball, Wiffle ball, or maybe even a Super Ball.

▶SETUP

- A player from each team meets on either side of the centerline for a face-off. The junkmaster or appointed assistant starts the face-off by throwing the ball between the two players.
- The rest of the players are on their sides of the centerline, facing the opponents.
- Each team has a goalie.

▶SAFETY

Players must wear shoes, even on the ice.

▶COACHING TIPS

- If the players want to remain more faithful to their understanding of hockey, you can include a penalty box and referee. Decide what things to penalize for. Make up some fun ones, like taking the game too seriously, falling down, being out of breath.

- If the players want to allow some kind of physical contact, add junk for making costumes: helmets, knee and elbow padding, and so on.

- There's an "official" game also called broom hockey, or broomball. This one is not it.

Noodle Hockey

Hockey with pool noodles and a beach ball.

The goal of the game is to get the beach ball through the opponent's goal. Players can only hit the ball with their noodles; they can't touch the ball with their hands. Yes, players can hit each other with the noodles as well (since it's inevitable, we might as well make it legal). Players cannot double up their noodles; they must hold them only by the middle and can use either end to hit the ball. The team with more goals at the end of 20 minutes wins.

▶ PLAYERS

Two teams of three to nine players per team.

▶ SPACE

The shallow end of a swimming pool or any open area at least 15 by 30 feet, even an ice rink.

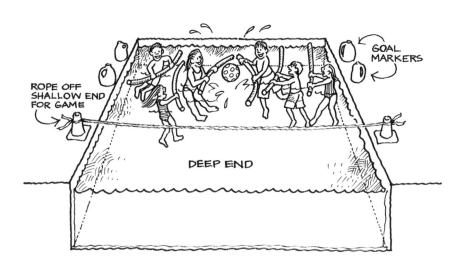

▶ JUNK

- A pool noodle for every player
- A beach ball
- Four traffic cones to use for making goals
- A rope to mark off the playing area so that the water is no deeper than the shortest player

▶ SETUP

- Find a pool.
- Mark off the deeper end of the playing area with the rope.
- Set up the goal markers on the left and right edges of the pool, with the markers about 3 feet apart in the middle of the width of the play area.

Do the following for other playing areas:

- Use tape to mark off an area at least 15 by 30 feet. Mark a midline.
- Give everyone a pool noodle.
- Start the game with a face-off between the two captains in the center of the playing area.

▶ SAFETY

Since most pool noodles are almost 5 feet long, players could be doing a lot of wide-range noodle whirling, especially in the water. That's why we suggest the rule that players hold their noodles by the middle. If players are having trouble with getting noodled, reduce the number of players.

▶ COACHING TIPS

Since this is what you might call a "soft war" game, do what you can to play up the fun of it. If people get too serious about the game, they might gang up on each other, which, though not necessarily painful, can be hurtful.

Frisbee Hockey

Hockey with a Frisbee for a puck.

The game is started with a face-off between the two captains facing each other along the centerline. Only the stick can touch the Frisbee. The Frisbee does not have to stay on the ground. Players score 1 point by getting the Frisbee to hit the opponent's trashcan. They score 5 points by getting the Frisbee to land inside the opponent's trashcan. The team with more points at the end of 20 minutes wins. No physical contact is allowed between players.

▶*PLAYERS*

Two teams of 3 to 11 players per team.

▶*SPACE*

A hockey rink, gym, playground, or protected street at least 15 by 45 feet.

▶*JUNK*

- A Frisbee for a puck
- Brooms, broom handles, or anything 2 to 3 feet long and sticklike that won't break (one for each player; you can use hockey sticks or even golf clubs)
- Tape or chalk to mark the centerline
- Two trashcans, one for each goal

▶*SETUP*

- Draw a centerline.
- Set up the goals on either end so that they're approximately 3 feet apart.

▶SAFETY

Players run with sticks, which is inherently unsafe. Slow the action down, or reduce the number of players if things start getting too serious. Since the Frisbee can be launched off the ground, players need to be aware that it could hit them.

▶COACHING TIPS

- Players get the most control and movement out of the Frisbee when the hollow side of the Frisbee is up and they can catch the lip of the Frisbee with the stick. This way, players push the Frisbee ahead of them. This also makes stick length less of a problem.

- It's almost impossible to get the Frisbee inside the trashcan unless two players work together, sandwiching it between their sticks.

Chariot Hockey

Play hockey while sitting down and getting pulled or pushed around.

Players, except for the goalies, get in pairs. One player is the driver, the other the stick handler, and one pair from each team begins the game with a traditional face-off. The goal is to score a point by getting the puck into the goal. Only the stick handler can touch the puck, and only with the stick. The puck must stay on the ground at all times. If it is lofted, the opposing team gains possession. Players change roles periodically (at every goal or at the direction of the junkmaster). No physical contact is allowed between players. The team with more points at the end of 20 minutes wins.

▶PLAYERS

Two teams of 6 to 22 players per team.

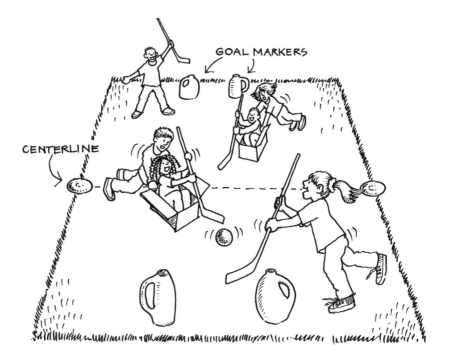

▶SPACE

Hockey rink, gym, or grassy field at least 15 by 45 feet. Set boundaries along the edges and a midline. Create goals at either end. Goals should be at least 3 feet wide.

▶JUNK

- Goals are trashcans, traffic cones, or milk bottles.
- The puck is a Frisbee, hockey puck, or sealed coffee can.
- Sticks are hockey sticks or brooms.
- Chariots are anything that slides (if playing on ice) or rolls and can be pushed or pulled: wheelchairs, sleds, tricycles, toboggans, cardboard cartons.

▶SETUP

- Players, except for the goalies, get in pairs. One player is the driver, the other the stick handler.
- One pair from each team begins the game with a traditional face-off.

▶SAFETY

Sitting players are closer to the stick, so be sure that players keep their sticks down. Perhaps playing with push brooms would be a safer alternative for some players. Be sure players practice pushing each other around so that they know how much effort to apply and can anticipate difficulties.

▶COACHING TIPS

This game is actually derived from sled hockey, a version of hockey developed for players with disabilities. Consequently, it can be readily adapted for players of mixed abilities.

Bumper Pool Hockey

Out-of-the-box hockey.

Players use their sticks to hit the tuna-can puck into the opponent's soda-can goal. Players can hit only the tuna can (not each other, not the goal cans, and not the obstacles), unless you want to make it a rule that they can hit the obstacles, which could have some interesting strategic implications. If you make that a rule, obstacles must not cross the boundary lines. Players must stand outside the boundaries. After someone scores, the obstacles must be reset in their original places. The player with more goals at the end of 20 minutes wins.

▶PLAYERS

Two to four players.

▶SPACE

An area at least 3 by 6 feet.

▶JUNK

- Obstacles are eight weighted coffee cans.
- Goals are two empty soda cans (one can for each goal).
- Boundaries are tape and six yardsticks.
- The puck is a tuna can.
- Sticks are two more yardsticks.

▶SETUP

- Lay out six yardsticks in a rectangle, one yard wide and two yards deep. Tape the sticks down.
- Place the soda-can goals at either end of the rectangle.
- Place the obstacles in three rows. In the rows closest to the front and back ends, place three obstacles. In the center, place two obstacles.
- Players take turns hitting the tuna-can puck.

▶ SAFETY

If the tuna-can puck flies around too easily, try using a sealed tuna can. Players must keep their sticks within the boundaries and stand outside them.

▶ COACHING TIPS

- Consider enlarging the court, making it for more players with bigger obstacles.

Air-Broom Hockey

Not air hockey, but hockey in the air.

The goal of this game is to get the balloon or beach ball into the trashcan goal without knocking the trashcans down. The ball must stay in the air at all times. If it hits the floor, the game stops, and a new face-off takes place at that point. The trashcans must not be knocked over. If they are knocked over by the team that owns the goal, the other team gets a free throw. If they are knocked over by the opposing team, a new face-off takes place at the centerline. Players, except for goalies, can hit the ball only with their brooms. Goalies can use anything handy. The team that gets more goals at the end of 20 minutes wins.

▶PLAYERS

Two teams of 3 to 11 players per team.

▶SPACE

An open field no smaller than 20 by 60 feet. An ice rink would be great, but it can be played in a gym or on a lawn or safe street. Goals are set up at each end of the field in the middle of the boundary line. A centerline is marked.

▶JUNK

- A broom for each player for the stick
- A balloon or beach ball for the puck
- Two trashcan towers of three trashcans each set up as goals so that the top one is mouth up
- Tape or chalk for the boundary lines

▶SETUP

- Captains of each team prepare for the face-off along the centerline.
- Players arrange themselves on their own side of the centerline.

▶SAFETY

People looking up at the ball can inadvertently run into each other. Remind the players to stay aware of their teammates' locations on the field.

▶COACHING TIPS

- If it's too hard to score, eliminate the position of goalie.
- If players are hitting each other with the brooms, purposefully or accidentally, take away the brooms and have them use their hands.

Hide-and-Seek Hockey

Hide, find, and hit the goal.

When the junkmaster or referee signals, the teams begin to move forward and try to find each other's goals (there is one per team), batting their ball as they go. Once the goal is placed, it cannot be moved. The ball can be touched only with the broom. The first team to find the goal and hit it with the ball scores. The team with more points at the end of 20 minutes wins. No physical contact is allowed between players.

▶ *PLAYERS*

Two teams of three to six players per team.

▶ *SPACE*

A network of hallways and corridors such as in a school or recreation center.

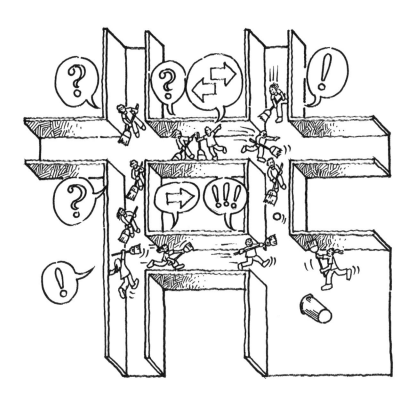

▶ JUNK

- For the puck, two Super Balls would be the most fun, but the least safe. Consider Ping-Pong or Wiffle balls or other small (3- to 6-inch), safe balls.
- Sticks are push brooms or regular brooms.
- The goal is a trashcan placed mouth down.

▶ SETUP

- The junkmaster or referee sets the goal somewhere in the agreed-on playing area. This is done in secret, out of visual range of the teams. But the goal must be in plain sight.
- Each team has a ball.

▶ SAFETY

Be sure that the area used is clear during playing time.

▶ COACHING TIPS

- Hiding the goal can be fun. Whoever does this needs to be reliably tight-lipped.
- Use as much of the building as is available to you (branching hallways, up and down stairs), but establish the limits of the playing area before you start the game, and be sure they are clear of nonplayers.
- Yes, teams can use (steal) each other's ball.
- It's a good strategy for a team to separate and send out scouts. By keeping the teams small, you make the strategy more challenging.
- When a goal is made, have the players yell "Goal!" (as in soccer) so that players who are far from the goal know what happened.

Chopsticky

Players can hit or lift and throw the ball between two sticks.

The goal of this game is to get the ball into the opponent's basket without knocking the trashcan tower over. Players can hit the ball or carry it between their two sticks. Players may not hit each other with the sticks. Players cannot run while carrying the ball. The trashcans must not be knocked over. If the team that owns the goal knocks over the trashcans, the other team gets a free throw. If the opposing team knocks them over, a new face-off takes place at the centerline. No physical contact is allowed between players.

▶*PLAYERS*

Two teams of 3 to 11 players per team.

▶*SPACE*

An ice rink, gym, playground or open field, at least 20 by 50 feet.

▶*JUNK*

- Two brooms (safer), yardsticks (lighter), or hockey sticks per player
- A small, light ball (Ping-Pong ball, Wiffle ball, 3- to 6-inch inflatable ball)
- Six trashcans or two basketball hoops
- Tape or chalk to mark the midline

▶*SETUP*

- Place a three-trashcan tower on each end of the playing field, with the top trashcan mouth up, or else a basketball hoop.
- Mark the centerline.
- Captains from each team meet for a face-off along the centerline.

▶*SAFETY*

Players will probably make use of their sticks for offense and defense. This means a lot of stick fights, which might mean that you'll need more referees. If so, have each team select one or two players to be referees. Make it a rule that if any player commits a foul, she has to change positions with a referee.

▶COACHING TIPS

- If stick fighting seems to be fun, but you're worried about it, have players tape sponges around the sticks and try the game again.
- Though the suggested rule is that players cannot run with the ball, you can always try it and see if it adds to the fun and skill of the game.
- If you're playing on a basketball court and you have baskets available to you, you might want to use a larger ball, but it still should be fairly light.

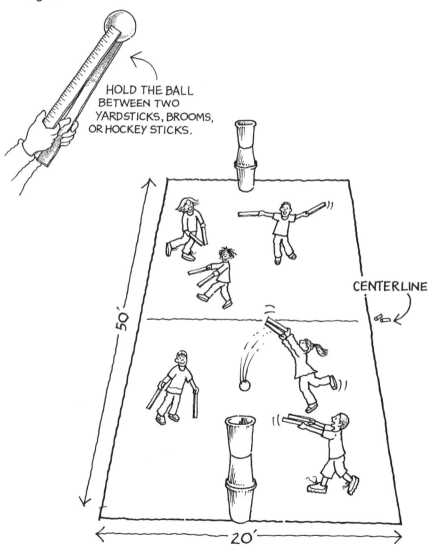

HOLD THE BALL BETWEEN TWO YARDSTICKS, BROOMS, OR HOCKEY STICKS.

CENTERLINE

50'

20'

Everybody Has a Ball Hockey

Competitive group juggling.

The junkmaster or referee has a bag of balls or pucks and drops the pucks, one at a time, into the face-off. The players in the face-off try to knock the ball or puck toward their team. Once the ball or puck is received, the team must keep that ball or puck in motion, passing it from player to player. A ball or puck that crosses a boundary is out of play and cannot be retrieved. Players from one team may attempt to get the ball away from the other team. Players may not touch each other physically with their sticks or with a ball.

The goal is to have as many balls as possible in play. The team that has more balls in play at the end of 10 minutes wins.

▶ *PLAYERS*

Two teams of 3 to 11 players per team.

▶ *SPACE*

An ice rink, gym, playground, or open field at least 20 by 20 feet.

▶ *JUNK*

- A ball or puck for every player (and maybe even a few more)
- A hockey stick or broom for each player

▶ *SETUP*

- All you need is a flat, open space with agreed-on boundaries.
- Players meet somewhere in the middle of the field.
- The captains are in position for the face-off.

▶ *SAFETY*

Caution players that balls or pucks must stay on the ground.

▶ *COACHING TIPS*

Shorten or lengthen the scoring intervals depending on how well everyone's playing. When the game is first played, have a scoring round every three minutes.

Shufflehockey

Shuffleboard with hockey sticks and pucks.

Players get the higher score by hitting the opponent's pucks out of the scoring area and hitting their own pucks so that they stop in the highest scoring area. With a pyramid target, the farthest zone counts as the most points, and the closest the fewest—usually 5, 10, and 20 points.

With a circular target, the center counts as the most points. Teams alternate turns and players. If a stick or broom crosses the shooting line, that team loses 15 points.

▶PLAYERS

Two teams of one to four players per team.

▶SPACE

An ice rink, gym, playground, alley, hallway, or open field at least 15 by 45 feet.

▶JUNK

- Four pucks per team
- A broom or hockey stick per team

▶SETUP

- Establish a shuffleboard-like target at one end of the playing area; use tape or chalk, if necessary, to mark it. The target can actually look like a target (two or three concentric rings) or like a pyramid divided into three horizontal bands.
- Establish a shooting line at least 35 feet away from the center of the target.

▶SAFETY

Just be sure that the space around the court is clear of nonplayers.

▶COACHING TIPS

When first playing, start with a practice round so that every player has at least one chance to get a feel for the game.

8.11 Bowl Hockey

Score as in bowling, play as in hockey.

The game begins with a face-off between two players, one from each team. The face-off is always done in the middle of the court along the centerline. Empty plastic soda bottles are lined up along the goal lines. The goal is to knock down all of the opposing team's soda bottles. Teams score 1 point for each soda bottle knocked down. The team with the higher score at the end of 20 minutes wins. Soda bottles can be hit only with the ball or puck. The ball or puck can be hit only by a broom or hockey stick. As soon as one or more bottles are knocked over, the game stops and the score is tallied. The bottles are reset and a new round begins with another face-off.

If a bottle is knocked over by a player (and not by the ball or puck), no score is counted. Again, the bottles are reset and a new round begins. Hitting another player with a stick is not allowed. No physical contact is allowed between players.

▶ *PLAYERS*

Two teams of 3 to 11 players per team.

▶ *SPACE*

An open field no smaller than 20 by 60 feet—an ice rink, gym, lawn, or safe street. Goals are set up at either end of the field in the middle of the front and back boundary line. A centerline is marked.

▶ *JUNK*

- 18 plastic liter soda bottles or plastic bowling pins
- One puck or small rubber or plastic ball (Wiffle ball)
- A hockey stick or broom for each player

▶ *SETUP*

- Place nine soda bottles in a diamond configuration approximately 15 feet from the back boundary (the goal zone) in the center. You want enough room so that players can move around all sides of the soda bottles.
- Mark the centerline and the boundary lines of the court.

▶ *SAFETY*

There's a lot of action, so it might be wise to appoint a player from each team to act as referee. As with other junkyard games, if a player commits a foul, she changes roles with a referee.

▶ *COACHING TIPS*

One goalie can't possibly protect the entire array of pins, so more than one player will have to play goalie for each team.

Puck Puck

Hockey with two pucks.

Both teams begin simultaneously by firing or passing the ball or puck toward their opponent's goal. Teams may steal each other's pucks. If a puck or ball crosses a boundary and remains across that boundary, it is out of play until a goal is scored or the other puck also crosses a boundary. The ball or puck must stay on the ground at all times.

As in all hockey games, players may not hit each other and may use their sticks or brooms only to hit the ball. No physical contact is allowed between players.

▶ PLAYERS

Two teams of 3 to 11 players per team.

▶ SPACE

An open field no smaller than 20 by 60 feet (an ice rink, gym, lawn, or safe street). Goals are set up at each end of the field in the middle of the front and back boundary line.

▶ JUNK

- Two hockey pucks or small, plastic balls
- A broom or hockey stick for each player
- Tape or chalk to mark the boundary lines
- Trashcans lying on their sides for goals (if there are no goal nets)

▶ SETUP

Players stand near their own goal zones, each team with its own puck or ball.

▶ SAFETY

Players need to be alert because there are essentially two hockey games going on at the same time. You might need to appoint referees to keep things safe.

▶ COACHING TIPS

- Remind players that they need to maintain both offense and defense at all times.
- If this game works well, consider adding two more pucks.

Skateboard Hockey 8.13

Hockey on skateboards.

The goal of this game is to get the puck into the opposing team's trashcan. Instead of having a face-off, start with one team in possession. Players (except for goalies) must have one foot on their skateboards at all times. Players must wear appropriate protective gear. It is illegal to hit another player with a stick or with the body. The ball or puck can be hit only with the stick. If the puck goes out of bounds, the other team gains possession. All play and movement must stop when a referee indicates a foul. The team with more goals at the end of 20 minutes wins.

▶PLAYERS

Two teams of 3 to 11 players per team.

▶SPACE

A street or paved area at least 20 by 50 feet.

▶JUNK

- Trashcans lying on their sides for goals
- Skateboards for all players except the goalies
- Helmets and knee and wrist pads for each player
- Hockey sticks or brooms for each player
- A street hockey puck or small ball

▶SETUP

- Place the trashcans on their sides, mouths facing inward, on either end of the playing area.
- Use chalk to mark the boundaries on all sides and a centerline.

▶SAFETY

This is by far the most dangerous game in this collection and should be treated as such. Each team should appoint two players to be referees.

▶COACHING TIPS

This game can be just as fun, and a lot safer, with everyone sitting on the skateboards.

CHAPTER 9

Junkyard Volleyball

Of all the team sports described in this book, volleyball lends itself best to the development of cooperative sports, in a junkyard-like sort of way. Even those games that aren't explicitly cooperative can be made, shall we say, "kind of" cooperative. For example, you know how teams are supposed to rotate every time they get the serve? Well, what would happen if we made it the rule that players rotate between teams? This way, everyone eventually winds up playing on both teams, which makes winning a shared victory and losing not so significant at all.

One other thing about net sports like volleyball is that you can use a fence for a net. I like this a lot, because it changes the function of a fence from something that separates people to something that brings them together.

Rally Volley

Play cooperatively. Count how many times you can get the ball over the net.

See how many times you can hit the ball back and forth across the net without dropping it. Play until the ball is dropped. The score for that round is the total number of hits. Rotate. Play again and see if you can beat the previous score. If there's only one player on a side, you have to hit the ball over the net each time you receive it. If there are two or more players, the same player can't hit the ball twice in a row.

▶ *PLAYERS*

Two teams of one to nine players per team.

▶ *SPACE*

The "official" volleyball court is about 30 by 60 feet and the height of the net from 6 to almost 8 feet. But these are junkyard sports, and volleyball is one of those sports that you can play just about anywhere. Usually the boundary lines are drawn around the space.

▶ *JUNK*

- For the net, if you don't have a volleyball net and poles to stretch it between, here are some alternatives: clothesline, with sheets for a net; socks, with socks for a net (make a chain of socks by tying them end to end, and dangle more socks from the chain for a "net effect"); rubber bands; or toilet paper. And if you don't have poles, you can use basketball stands, brooms, trees, or lampposts.
- For the ball, a beach ball or some light, easy-to-hit ball is all you really need, though having some other volleyable balls around wouldn't hurt.

▶ *SETUP*

- Two players or teams stand on opposite sides of the net. The net is in the center of the playing area.
- The field should be at least 20 by 30 feet if you have nine players on a side.

▶ *SAFETY*

Be sure that the field is fairly level and free of obstacles. Keep nonplayers far enough away from the field so that no one runs into them or hits them with the ball.

▶ *COACHING TIPS*

- No boundary lines are needed, unless you're playing in a crowded area and need to keep passers-by safe.
- Though it is better if players adhere to basic volleyball practices (the ball has to be hit over the net after the third tap), it is not essential for this game.
- If players get bored with this, encourage them to develop other routines. Use the Harlem Globetrotters as an example. Bring a boom box for music. Have them run in circles, run between sides, square dance, whatever seems like more fun.

Kingvolley

A combination of four square and volleyball.

As in volleyball, the goal is to hit the ball so that it goes into the other team's territory. If the other team fails to return the ball, the serving team gets a point and keeps the serve. If the serving team does not complete an acceptable serve, or if the ball is returned to the serving team and not returned again, the next team, counterclockwise from the serving team, gets the serve. The ball must bounce once on the server's side, clear the net, and then bounce once on any of the other three sides before it is returned. The ball may be hit by as many as three people on each team, and no player may hit the ball twice in succession. Players can stand and return the ball when they are outside the boundaries as long as the ball has hit their square. The team with more points at the end of 20 minutes wins.

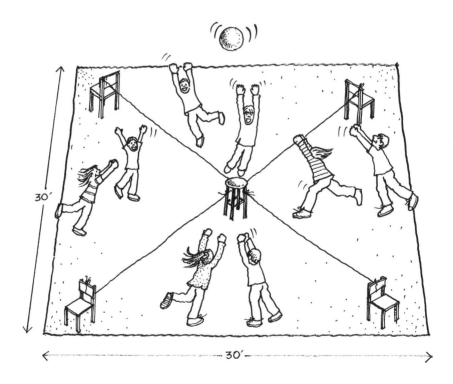

▶PLAYERS

Four teams of one to six players per team.

▶SPACE

A clear space, about 30 by 30 feet, on a hard surface, divided into four spaces of 15 by 15 feet each by two intersecting nets. The nets are 2 to 8 feet high.

▶JUNK

- Use chalk to draw boundaries around the four edges of the court.
- Nets are toilet paper and stools, or chairs and ribbon, or four volleyball nets and five volleyball net posts.
- For a ball, use a good playground ball with a high bounce, maybe even a smaller volleyball (6 inches in diameter).

▶SETUP

- If the players have the requisite sense of humor, you can make two intersecting nets with toilet paper strung between stools—five stools, each turned upside down, one in the center, the rest radiating from the center stool, toilet paper taped to one of the legs.
- Use chalk to draw the boundaries around the edges of the court.

▶SAFETY

Since the play goes beyond the confines of the "box," it is advisable to keep an additional 10 feet clear around the perimeter.

▶COACHING TIPS

- You might want to start the game with fewer players and add more as people get the idea of the game.
- Encourage players to add any rules they know from four square and volleyball that might make the game more fun.

Water Balloony

Arm volleyball players with water balloons.

A regulation game of volleyball is played, complete with volleyball and net. The only difference is that each player also has a water balloon that they can use offensively or defensively to distract the players on the other team. A player may throw her water balloon over the net at any time. If another player can catch the water balloon, he may do so. Play continues as in normal volleyball, with the serving team scoring a point every time the opposing team can't return a fair ball. The team with more points at the end of 20 minutes wins.

▶ PLAYERS

Two teams of one to nine players per team.

▶ SPACE

An outdoor waterproof volleyball court, playground, park, lawn, beach, or vacant parking lot.

▶ JUNK

- Balloons filled with water
- Volleyball or playground ball
- Rope and pins, chalk, socks, toilet paper for boundary lines
- Chalk, a volleyball net on posts, or some clever substitute (clothesline and sheets strung between posts, or maybe just a fence somewhere) for the net

▶ SETUP

- Find a place where you can play volleyball and that can also get wet.
- Give every player a water balloon.

▶*SAFETY*

Play on a warm day. People might get water in their eyes, so have some towels around. Watch out for mud and slippery puddles.

▶*COACHING TIPS*

- This game is more for fun than for score, but trying to do both turns out to be more fun.
- Remember, balloons can be caught, but volleyballs can't. This adds to the confusion and skill.
- Encourage players to develop strategies for sharing water balloons with their team.

Towely Volley

Kind of a blanket-toss game for volleyballs.

As in volleyball, the goal is to cause the other team to miss a legal serve. Pairs must keep their hands on their towel at all times. The ball may be tossed among players on the same team up to three times before it must be lofted over the net. The ball should be returned more or less immediately after being caught. The players can't touch the ball with their hands. The team with more points at the end of 20 minutes wins.

▶ PLAYERS

Two teams of 2 to 18 players per team (in pairs).

▶ SPACE

Volleyball court, indoors or out.

▶ JUNK

- At least one towel for every two players
- A volleyball, playground ball, or even a ball made out of towels and tape
- A net, fence, or clothesline

SNAP!

▶ SETUP

- Players stand in pairs, facing each other, holding on to the ends of a towel.
- The serving team has the ball.
- A pair gets into position behind the rear boundary line and snaps the towel to launch the ball over the net.

▶ SAFETY

It's challenging for players who are holding on to a towel to coordinate their movements, so there's more likelihood for people to run into each other accidentally.

▶ COACHING TIPS

- There are a lot of unusual circumstances to explore with this game, so consider starting with a 5-minute volley as a practice session and then asking the players for words of advice about how to play the game.
- It can be played with four on a towel. It can be played with blankets. It can be played with parachutes.

Gollyball

Get the ball as high as possible.

The goal of this game is to get the ball as high as possible for as long as possible. Everyone wins when everyone is amazed at how high they got the ball, and how long they were able to keep it that way, given the 20-minute time limit. Players hit the ball as high as possible—no spiking or overhand hits. Players keep the ball going for as long as possible. When the ball is not returned, players rotate between teams. The player who last served for Team A takes the position of the net player on the left for Team B. Team B's player who was in the serving position becomes the leftmost net player for Team A. Once all of the rotating is completed, Team B serves.

▶ PLAYERS

Two teams of one to nine players per team.

▶ SPACE

Any reasonably flat area, at least 30 by 30 feet, divided by a net or fence.

▶ JUNK

- Volleyball, playground ball, or beach ball
- Fence or net made out of clothesline, rope, anything

▶ SETUP

The higher you can make the net, the better. It's not absolutely necessary that the net be higher than usual, but it helps.

▶ SAFETY

Players are looking up most of the time, so they're more likely to run into each other.

▶ COACHING TIPS

As players become more proficient in this game, encourage them to try other tricks:

- Rotate within or between teams while the ball is in the air.
- Give each other high fives while the ball is in the air.
- Sit down and stand up.

Goodminton

Volleyball with rackets and smaller balls.

The birdie must be hit over the net and fall within the opposing team's boundaries. A team may hit the birdie up to three times before hitting it over the net. The serving team scores when the receiving team is unable to legally return the birdie so that it would land within the boundaries of the other team's side. If the serving team fails to return a fairly returned birdie, the other team gains the serve. No overhand swings. No spiking. The team with more points at the end of 20 minutes wins.

▶**PLAYERS**

Two teams of one to nine players per team.

▶**SPACE**

A volleyball court.

▶**JUNK**

- A few badminton birdies, shuttlecocks, or Schmerltzes made out of a short sock and maybe a Ping-Pong ball
- If needed, materials to mark boundary lines (tape, chalk, rope, ribbon)
- Any kind of racket (tennis racket, badminton racket, squash racket, or even a Ping-Pong paddle), one for each player
- A volleyball net strung between two poles, or equivalent (clothesline with sheets draped over it, a fence, and the like)

▶**SETUP**

- Teams stand on either side of the net, each player with a racket.
- String the net as high as possible.

▶**SAFETY**

Players should be encouraged to stay within their position. Because they each have a racket, moving around and swinging could be hazardous.

▶**COACHING TIPS**

If it's too hard to score, consider adding another birdie or several, or consider changing the overhand and spiking rule.

Handless Volley

Play volleyball without using your hands.

Players may use any part of their body, other than their hands, to return the ball. All the rules of volleyball are in play: Players on a team can hit the ball up to three times before hitting it over the net; no player may hit the ball twice in succession; the ball is served from behind the serving team's back boundary; teams rotate when the defending team fails to return the ball; the serving team scores if the opposing team can't return a fairly served ball. The team with the higher score at the end of 20 minutes wins.

▶ *PLAYERS*

Two teams of one to six players per team.

▶ *SPACE*

A hard or soft volleyball court (concrete, wood, dirt, or sand), at least 30 by 30 feet, bisected by a net.

▶ *JUNK*

- A balloon or beach ball, or plastic (Wiffle) ball, or sock ball
- A volleyball, tennis, or badminton net or a rope, string, or length of toilet paper

▶SETUP

- If possible, the net is set at badminton height (5 feet) or lower (maybe 3 feet).
- Teams stand on either side of the net.

▶SAFETY

Players can use their feet to kick the ball, which means that they can kick each other. That's why the suggested maximum team size is six. Be sure players stand well away from each other in assigned positions.

▶COACHING TIPS

- You might consider introducing this demonstration game by using a balloon so that players can practice and develop control. When players are ready for more of a challenge, consider using a heavier ball with less bounce.
- This demonstration game is loosely based on a real sport, called takraw, which is played in Indonesia.

Netless Volley

Players bounce a ball into each other's court.

The ball must bounce on both sides of the net lines to be considered fair. The serving team bounces the ball down on their side of the court so that it bounces over the net lines and hits the other side. If the ball bounces only on one side and then lands out of bounds, or if the ball bounces on or between the net lines, the other team gets the serve. The ball can only be hit down—when players within a team pass the ball to each other, it must bounce first before the other player can return it. All other rules of volleyball are in effect. The serving team gets a point every time the receiving team fails to return a fairly served ball. The team with more points at the end of 20 minutes wins.

▶PLAYERS

Two teams of one to nine players per team.

▶SPACE

Any hard-surfaced area (playground, gym, parking lot) about 30 by 30 feet.

▶JUNK

- A 3- to 8-inch ball with good bounce (a mini-volleyball or soccer ball, a "pinkie" ball)
- Chalk for drawing boundary markers

▶SETUP

- Divide the court in half. Draw two lines, about three feet apart, along that division.
- Teams stand on either side of the lines.

▶SAFETY

Players should be sure to leave enough space between them so that the ball can be bounced. This can cause some minor accidents as players back into each other.

▶COACHING TIPS

- Encourage players to experiment with control over the ball (imparting spin, bouncing low, and the like).
- If it's too easy for the serving team to score, widen the net lines and shrink the boundaries.

Chair Volley

Play volleyball while sitting in a chair.

Players must be seated before they hit the ball; they may be standing at other times. If the net is torn, the team that tore the net loses either the serve or a point. All other rules of volleyball apply except that there should be no spiking allowed. The serving side scores a point every time the receiving team fails to return a fairly served ball. The side with more points at the end of 20 minutes wins.

▶PLAYERS

Two teams of one to nine players per team.

▶SPACE

Any paved or carpeted surface with an open area of 30 by 30 feet.

▶JUNK

- Beach ball or volleyball
- One chair per player, plus a couple of chairs to make net posts
- Clothesline or toilet paper and tape to make the net

▶SETUP

- Place chairs in the positions where players would stand, one for each player.
- Place two chairs in the position of the net poles and tape a length of toilet paper between them for the net.

▶SAFETY

Getting up and then sitting down while in the heat of trying to get in position to hit a ball can be hazardous. If it seems like it could become a problem, make it a rule that players must remain seated except when rotating.

▶COACHING TIPS

- Start with the beach ball until people get the feel for the game.
- This game is appropriate for players of mixed abilities.
- Try playing with one or two players unseated.

Living-Room Volley

Play volleyball indoors with a balloon.

See how long you can keep the balloon in play before it hits the ground. Players are not allowed to stand. They may kneel, sit, or crawl. The ball may not be tapped more than three times by one side, and not twice in succession by any one player. Play in 5-minute intervals and see if players can beat their scores.

▶*PLAYERS*

Two teams of one to three players per team.

▶*SPACE*

A living room with fragile things stored in places where they can't get knocked over.

▶*JUNK*

- Balloons for the ball (maybe five)
- Toilet paper, or a couch, for the net

▶SETUP

- If there's enough room, use the sofa for the net.
- If there's not enough room, string some toilet paper between two chairs or something else.
- If there's still not enough room, use the doorway and have players on opposite sides of the door.
- Players sit on the floor on either side of the net.

▶SAFETY

Do your best to make sure that the area is free of fragile things like glass, china, and babies.

▶COACHING TIPS

Try this with several balloons at a time.

Volleyall

Everybody has a ball, netlessly.

Players begin with one ball, and the ball must be hit up into the air and to another player. When anyone asks for another ball, the junkmaster throws it into the circle. A ball that is dropped is out of play until the junkmaster retrieves it and throws it back in. No one other than the junkmaster may hold a ball; the ball must be constantly volleyed. The goal of this game is to keep as many balls as possible in the air at the same time. Play in two 10-minute intervals. See if players can beat their scores (the number of balls in motion when the time is up).

▶ *PLAYERS*

From 2 to 20 players.

▶ *SPACE*

Any open space, 10 to 20 feet in diameter, depending on how many play-ers there are.

▶ *JUNK*

Use a beach ball for each player (or a balloon, or playground ball, or vol-leyball).

▶ *SETUP*

Players stand in a circle.

▶ *SAFETY*

There are few safety concerns, other than making sure the area is clear of obstacles.

▶ *COACHING TIPS*

- If players start moving around, it can make the game more fun and more chaotic.
- If playing with players of mixed abilities, consider having all players seated (either on chairs or on the floor).

Volleyvolley

Play volleyball in two directions simultaneously.

Both teams serve simultaneously. Players on the same team can tap the ball up to five times (as long as no player hits the same ball twice in a row) before they have to tap it over the net. When one team misses, the other team scores and both teams rotate. A team gets a point when the other team fails to return the serve. The team with more points at the end of 20 minutes wins.

▶**PLAYERS**

Two teams of one to nine players per team.

▶**SPACE**

Volleyball court (indoors or outdoors), tennis court, badminton court, or any open space about 30 by 30 feet, divided in half by a net.

▶**JUNK**

- A volleyball and a playground ball
- Something for a net if needed (rope or yarn)

▶**SETUP**

- Each team stands on opposite sides of the net.
- Each team has a ball.

▶**SAFETY**

With both balls in motion, there's a greater chance that people will run into each other.

▶**COACHING TIPS**

- There should be a lot of scoring. If not, consider allowing players to spike the ball (there's no rule against it).
- With the added amount of passes allowed, one team can have two balls going. This can be very strategic.

Schmerltz Volley

Schmerltz-throwing volleyball.

The Schmerltz is always thrown underhand, usually twirled by the sock end and then flung. A receiving player must catch the Schmerltz by the tail and then immediately throw it.

The Schmerltz can be thrown to another player on the same team, but it must be thrown to the other team by the third throw. When the serving team misses or does not follow any of these rules, the other team gains possession. The goal of the serving team is to throw a Schmerltz that the receiving team can't catch, and therefore gain a point. The team with more points at the end of 20 minutes wins.

▶PLAYERS

Two teams of 1 to 20 players per team.

▶SPACE

Any open field at least 30 by 60 feet.

▶JUNK

- A few Schmerltzes (a knee sock with a tennis ball tied into the toe)
- Toilet paper, ribbon, or rope for boundaries

▶SETUP

- A line is made in the middle of the field.
- Teams stand anywhere on either side of the line.

▶SAFETY

There's a lot of running in this game, so be sure that the space is open, free of obstacles, and clear of nonplayers.

▶COACHING TIPS

- Practice throwing and catching the Schmerltz by the tail before playing competitively.
- If necessary, reduce the size of the playing area.
- Be sure that players understand what it means to catch and throw without pausing.

Resources

The Junkyard Sports Web site is at www.junkyardsports.com. It was set up specifically to share descriptions, photos, and videos of new junkyard sports. If you are interested in seeing what others are doing, or want to contribute your own ideas, this will be your ongoing resource.

The author's Web site, www.deepfun.com, contains a great deal of background information about games and play as well as many links to more resources. For a good collection of noncompetitive games similar to those used in New Games, see his collection of "pointless" (without score) games at www.deepfun.com/pointless.html.

Though The New Games Foundation no longer exists, Dale LeFevre, at www.inewgames.com, is doing a great job at keeping the spirit of New Games alive. A great background source for the foundation of junkyard sports is a somewhat nostalgic site called Streetplay at www.streetplay.com. Here's where you'll find games like Boxball, Skully, and Stickball. It's a great inspiration and validation for more junkyard sports.

About the Author

Bernie DeKoven is serious about having fun and about helping others have fun, too. He has been reinventing sports for more than 35 years, has designed a curriculum with more than 1,000 children's games, and has developed the training program for The New Games Foundation. The concept of New Games has had a worldwide effect on physical education and recreation. Along the way he designed and led an event for 250,000 people for the Philadelphia Bicentennial celebration, where he introduced Really Big Pick-Up Sticks (16 feet long) and Big, Big Box Blocks.

DeKoven, who has an MA in theater from Villanova University, has invented almost every kind of game—educational, entertainment, digital, physical, social, mental—for companies such as Mattel Toys and the Children's Television Workshop. He is a lifetime member of the Association for the Study of Play. To learn more about junkyard sports (and to see some examples of it in action), visit his Web site at www.junkyardsports.com. To contact DeKoven about workshops (which are guaranteed to be instructive, creative, and above all, *fun)*, e-mail DeKoven at bernie@dekoven.com.

About the Illustrator

Bob Gregson is an artist who combines art and play. For over 30 years, Gregson has organized innovative events that encourage collective creativity for people of all ages. His large-scale public celebrations bring diverse communities together with such events as the Special Olympics World Games, First Night, and OpSail. Gregson received his master of fine arts degree from the Art Institute of Chicago and has worked for museums and nonprofit art organizations. He is currently the creative director for the State of Connecticut Tourism Division. As an artist he uses architectural elements, photography, and community planning to design projects that invite an interactive dialogue. His first meeting with Bernie DeKoven in the 1970s opened new creative vistas resulting in a citywide "Play Day" attracting 10,000 playful participants in Hartford, Connecticut. He is the author and illustrator of several popular games books for teachers—linking arts, games, and education in unique relationships. You can learn more about Gregson by visiting his Web site at www.BobGregson.com.

*You'll find
other outstanding
sports resources at*

www.HumanKinetics.com

In the U.S. call

1-800-747-4457

Australia..............................	08 8372 0999
Canada	1-800-465-7301
Europe......................	+44 (0) 113 255 5665
New Zealand...................	0064 9 448 1207

HUMAN KINETICS
The Information Leader in Physical Activity
P.O. Box 5076 • Champaign, IL 61825-5076 USA